Visitor's
FLOR

GW00501476

*The Author*

The author is an American who has travelled widely in his native country. After 4 years 'touring' America with the Air Force, he spent 10 years marketing computer systems in Britain. In 1989 Brian formed a travel writing team with his British photographer-fiancée, Jackie, who recieved her first photography award aged 10. They have negotiated 30,000 miles of American Highway (including 6,000 miles in Florida to research this guide) in their motorhome, and will soon have re-visited every state in the USA.

ALABAMA

GEORGIA

ATLANTIC OCEAN

• Crestveiw
PENSACOLA • Marianna
Panama City •
CHAPTRER 8  • TALLAHASSEE

• JACKSONVILLE
Lake City
CHAPTER 7   • St Augustine

• GAINESVILLE

• Ocala   • Daytone Beach

• Titusville
ORLANDO •

GULF OF MEXICO

TAMPA •
ST PETERSBURG •   • MELBOURNE
CHAPTER 5
• Sarasota   • Fort Pierce
CHAPTER 4   CHAPTER 6

Fort Myers •   • PALM BEACH
CHAPTER 3
Naples •   FORT LAUDERDALE

MIAMI
CHAPTER 1

0          100 miles
0          200 km

N

FLORIDA

CHAPTER 2   FLORIDA KEYS

# VISITOR'S GUIDE:
# FLORIDA

**Brian Merritt**

## MPC
## HUNTER
PUBLISHING INC

Cover photograph:
Launch of the Orbiter Space Shuttle
from Cape Canaveral *(Florida
Division of Tourism).*

Published by:
Moorland Publishing Co Ltd,
Moor Farm Road West,
Ashbourne,
Derbyshire DE6 1HD
England

ISBN 0 86190 451 6 (paperback)

Published in the USA by:
Hunter Publishing Inc,
300 Raritan Center Parkway,
CN 94, Edison, NJ 08818

ISBN 1 55650 474 8 (USA)

British Library Cataloguing in
Publication Data:
A catalogue record for this book is
available from the British Libraray

Colour origination by
Scantrans, Singapore

Printed in the UK by:
Richard Clay Ltd. Bungay, Suffolk

Illustrations have been supplied by:
Busch Gardens: 71 top; Breakers Resort: 127; Daytona CVB: 15 top, 142;
Discovery Center: 123 lower; Flagler
Museum: 130 lower; Florida Division of Tourism: 158 top; Greater
Miami CVB: 23 top, 26, 27 right;
Jackie: 27 left, 31, 55 left, 59 top, 63, 71
lower, 79 lower, 123 top, 130 top, 139,
147, 155 left; Leon County CVB: 155
right, 158 lower; Miami Seaquarium:
23 lower; Newman Associates: 19,
42, 46, 50; NPS by Tom Cawley: 55
right; NPS by Williams: 59 lower;
Orlando/Orange CVB: 115; Palm
Beach CVB: 126; Pensacola C of C:
163; Pinellas CVB: 74, 79 top, 87; Sea
World of Florida: 11, 107 top; Space
Coast CVB: 15 lower; Universal Studios Florida: 107 lower; The Walt
Disney Company: 95, 99, 103

## Acknowledgments

The author is indebted to the following for their assistance in compiling
this guide: The Florida Division of
Tourism (Rosetta Land & Michelle);
Florida Department of Natural Resources (Bill Egan & Joe Knowles),
Alice McDaniels, Newman Associates, Tampa CVB, Naples C of C
(Sue), TW Recreation, Fort Myers
Historical Society, the Florida room
at Tallahassee Library, and the National Parks Service. Also Jackie, an
observant, artistic and huggable
photographer, who can also bake,
drive a motorhome, run an appointment and reminder service, and
stand four months of non-stop travel
with me.

# *CONTENTS*

|   | Introduction | 7 |
| 1 | Greater Miami | 20 |
| 2 | The Florida Keys | 38 |
| 3 | The Everglades | 53 |
| 4 | Tampa and the Gulf Coast | 68 |
| 5 | Orlando: the Heart of Florida | 93 |
| 6 | The Gold Coast | 120 |
| 7 | North-East Florida: the Gateway to Space | 136 |
| 8 | The Panhandle | 153 |
|   | Florida Fact File | 169 |
|   | Index | 189 |

## Key to Symbols Used in Text and on Maps

 Recommended walk

 Archaeological or historical site

 Nature reserve/animal interest

 Garden

 Park*/recreational area

 Church

 Building of interest

 Castle or fortification

 Museum or art gallery

 Other place of interest

 Birdlife

 Marine or underwater interest

 Boating and boat trips

 Accessible to the handicapped

*Parks in Florida often include beaches, walks, swimming, marine life, birdlife, boating, camping and a visitor centre, so the symbol belies their wide diversity of interests.

## Key to Maps

═══ Toll Highway

▬▬▬ Interstate Highway

══ US Highway

▬▬ County Road

City/town

Lake/river

─ ─ ─ State Boundary

─ ─ ─ ─ National Park Boundary

S/P State Park    S/R/A State Recreational Area

### Note on the maps
The maps drawn for each chapter, while comprehensive, are not designed to be used as route maps, but rather to locate the main cities, towns and places of interest.

# *INTRODUCTION*

F lorida beckons the traveller with images of sunshine and beaches, with Magic Kingdoms and a gateway to space. The sunshine and climate is legendary, and the beaches boast household names, like Miami, Palm, and Daytona. The technological showcase at Kennedy Space Center pauses only for launches, while, at Walt Disney World, daily cares are left far behind.

## The Nature of Florida

This magical montage of sunny Florida is all a holidaymaker could desire, and the vision is not far from reality. But there is another Florida that also beckons, a natural wonderland awaiting discovery.

Bubbling up throughout northern and central Florida are more than 300 clear springs. Run off from the Appalachian Mountains and points south percolate through the earth, dissolving passages through Florida's deep limestone foundation. Immense pressures force out this crystal water, which flows year-round at the same temperature — refreshingly cool in summer yet pleasantly warm in winter. Waterways are everywhere — you can go 'way down upon' the Suwannee River, or take a paddle-wheeler up the St Johns, the largest north-flowing river in America. A host of rivers and streams offer boating, fishing, and canoeing. Over 4,000 square miles of Florida is water, formed by the tens of thousands of lakes, waterways and streams. Florida is a water enthusiast's heaven on earth.

Everyone knows of the Everglades, that wild mixture of habitats which co-exist to form a most complex, sensitive ecosystem. Impenetrable coastal mangrove swamps give way to broad savannahs of grass and saw palmettos, peppered by hardwood islands called hammocks. The scarcely moving waterways would soon silt up but for the relentless efforts of the alligator, whose reward is a water hole filled with tasty companions during the dry months. At these times sections of the Everglades could be mistaken for a desert, and the fish that congregate in pools become food for Florida's rich and varied bird population.

Many exotic birds, such as the roseate spoonbill and snowy egret, share the coastal Everglades with the osprey, pelican, and great herons. The mockingbird is the Florida state bird, a greyish songbird which flashes a beacon of white while flying. Visitors commonly mistake the identity of the great birds which can often be seen soaring in lazy circles. Large birds with broad wings held in a 'V' are black or turkey vultures. Should the wings be slightly swept back and flatter, look closely for the symbol of America, the bald eagle.

The waterways abound with innumerable fish, despite being pursued by heron, egrets, fishermen, otter and, of course, the alligator. Having been hunted for centuries the alligator is now coming back in greater numbers. Visitors are asked not to feed the wildlife, lest the animals associate humans with food.

One Florida resident, an ancient cousin of the elephant, is becoming increasingly rare. The delightful manatee spends its life improving Florida's waterways by clearing the vegetation, with few thanks from careless boaters. In winter manatees congregate at sources of warmth, such as power stations, or the constant temperatures of the larger springs. At Blue Springs State Park, for example, sixty or more may be spotted on wintry mornings. Manatees can always be found north of Tampa at Homosassa Springs, at EPCOT Center in The Living Seas, or at Miami Seaquarium, Lowry Zoo, and Sea World. The latter three are most commendable.

Natural Florida is an important timber and paper producer. In addition to privately owned lands there are huge national and state forests, which combine resource management with public access and recreation. White tailed deer populate the forests and even the occasional black bear. Visitors are much more likely to spot squirrels, woodpeckers, mourning doves, raccoons and perhaps a 'possum during the evening. Florida's highest northern peak, at nearly 350ft, it will impress few mountaineers, but at least it dispels the myth of Florida being *entirely* flat.

The 1,300 miles of shore line includes some 800 miles of beach. From Georgia a chain of barrier islands stretch down the Atlantic Coast, with beaches of fine quartz sand. Separating the islands from the mainland are marshlands rich in wildlife and also canals, the granddaddy of them all being the Intracoastal Waterway. Barges bound for New York from Texas (and vice versa) share this enhanced natural canal with sailing yachts and low, sleek bass boats with massive outboard motors. Driving is a popular pastime on Daytona Beach, and some of the best surfing is between Cocoa Beach and Fort Lauderdale. The Florida surf may lack the glamour of the Banzai Pipeline, but a surfer has to start somewhere.

The Keys are an archipelago of stepping stones running from Miami's doorstep towards the middle of the Gulf of Mexico, ending in the dots called the Dry Tortugas. Following the Atlantic coastline from south Florida down to the Keys is the only living coral reef off continental American shores, fed by the rich waters of the Bermuda Channel. Indeed, many Keys are ancient coral reefs. Nature provided few beaches at the Keys, but man has since put that score right.

Beyond the 10,000 mangrove islands of the Everglades estuaries is Florida's Gulf of Mexico coastline. The southernmost sections are renowned for fine sand, while St Petersburg and Clearwater Beaches are packed with activities. Beyond Tarpon Springs the beaches fade away, re-emerging with a vengeance at the best stretch of 'sugar sand' in Florida. Often called the Emerald Coast, the white beach and topaz water runs from St George Island, near Tallahassee, across the panhandle to Pensacola.

## Florida's Changing Fortunes

The first aboriginals reached panhandle Florida some 10,000 years ago. The paleo-Indians enjoyed a rich and diverse diet, with typical inland fare supplemented by the teeming life within Florida's swamps, rivers, estuaries, and lakes. Through trade with Central and South America the hunter-gatherers learned agriculture. They built increasingly complex mounds, which were abandoned shortly before contact with the Europeans. By the arrival of the Spanish, the Indians were living two distinctly different lifestyles. The northern Timucua and Apalachee Indians had a high degree of civilization, with palisades protecting their homes, and their lands were extensively cultivated. Agriculture was also attempted in southern Florida, but the swampy earth was prone to flooding. The Ais, Tekesta, and Calusa returned to a hunter-gatherer lifestyle.

Juan Ponce de Leon, who came to the New World on the second Columbus voyage, is credited as Europe's dramatic discoverer of Florida. He sailed from Puerto Rico in search of gold and silver, spices, pearls and slaves. He discovered a distinctive jutting peninsula (believing it to be another island) while searching for Bimini, of which he was promised the governorship. The date was early April 1513, six days after the crew had celebrated Easter's Pascua Florida (Feast of Flowers), which the new land was named after. Six months later Ponce de Leon returned to Puerto Rico to prepare for another foray. The riches were rumoured to be just inland, but first Ponce needed more men at arms as the local Indians were decidedly hostile to the Spanish.

Ponce de Leon's second expedition was delayed when he was ordered to put down a Carib Indian uprising. In the meantime, other explorers stirred trouble along Florida's shores by enslaving local Indians. Fate, in the guise of an arrow, struck Ponce shortly after his return to Florida. Fired by an immensely powerful bow, the Indian's wood-tipped arrows splintered, thus piercing even the finest chain mail. Ponce de Leon and his ships returned to Cuba, where he died.

The next expedition fared less well. Navarez set sail from Spain with 600 followers, and landed near present day Tampa. Lured inland by tales of silver, he and 300 men hacked their way across Florida, to find only hostile Indians. A dejected Navarez returned to the coast near present day St Marks, but the supply ships sent to meet them never arrived. In the wilderness the survivors reforged their armour into tools and nails, and built five wooden boats. With sails made from their clothing they headed for Mexico, but the over-loaded boats capsized in a storm. Amazingly, four of the men reached shore and endured a seven-year trek to Mexico City. Their ordeal proved that Florida was connected with North America.

Hernando de Soto was the last of the great *conquistadors* to attack Florida. He also arrived near Tampa with some 600 knights, soldiers and slaves. By a coincidence he spent his first winter in the present day boundaries of Tallahassee, where he celebrated 'America's First Christmas'. For several years De Soto blazed a twisted path across America, but the cities of gold were always just beyond the next hill. When he fell ill and died, his body was placed in the Mississippi River to prevent Indian desecration. Although De Soto failed to discover treasure, his expedition brought back the first real under-standing of the capital and manpower required to colonize Florida. Further exploration was postponed while the more lucrative Central and South American civilizations were milked of their riches.

The Spanish were beginning to realize that murder, enslavement, and torture were not always productive. A more effective method of civilizing the Indians was deemed necessary, and the priesthood suggested missionaries. Father Louis Cancer de Barbastro was the first martyr, whose well planned scheme of finding Indians un-touched by earlier atrocities was ruined by a callous navigator who brought him to Tampa Bay, landing site of the Navarez and De Soto expeditions. He knelt to thank God for a safe arrival in Florida, and was beheaded by Indians before uttering a word.

Meanwhile infighting between Catholics and the Protestant Huguenots was tearing France apart. The New World was seductive to the troubled French, offering wealth and a colony where the Huguenots could begin anew. Admiral Jean Ribaut explored the Florida coast in 1562, and two years later Fort Caroline was established on the St Johns River. In time the colony might have contended for Florida, but it was dealt a blow by dissatisfied colonists. A group of adventurers had come for promised riches and, finding none, absconded in a ship and began to plunder the Spanish.

Imperial Spain was decidedly sensitive regarding pirates. The trade winds blew along the coast of Florida, and becalmed treasure ships could be attacked by reckless buccaneers in rowboats. Unaware of the Fort Caroline settlement until they captured the French

*A manatee being cared for at Sea World before being released into the wild*

deserters, Spain learned that many settlers were Protestants. To the Catholic Spaniards heresy was a far greater crime than piracy.

Ribaut was aware of a growing Spanish Armada, and hastily gathered his own fleet. The Spaniards attacked under the leadership of Pedro Menendez de Aviles. Finding Ribaut's fleet assembled outside Fort Caroline, Menendez sailed south to establish a Spanish settlement named St Augustine. Ribaut boldly set sail to attack the entrenching Spanish, but was struck by a hurricane. His fleet was destroyed and he and several groups of his men were washed ashore south of St Augustine. Meanwhile, Menendez just as boldly marched up the coast and captured the sleeping Fort Caroline. The non-Catholic majority, excepting musicians, were put to death. Later, Indians brought news of French survivors and Menendez convinced a group of them to surrender. There were too many prisoners to hold safely, so the non-Catholic majority were again put to death. Ribaut and his group refused to surrender, and fought the Spaniards, but without success. Ribaut was beheaded, his remaining men enslaved, and the blood stained beach has since born the name Matanzas (Slaughter). Dominique de Gourgues sailed from France and pillaged San Mateo, as Fort Caroline was renamed by the Spanish, hanging the Catholic soldiers and settlers. Thus avenged, France concentrated her efforts in the north, far from Spanish Territory, until the Mississippi River brought them south to New Orleans.

St Augustine was untouched by the dispute with France, and the Spaniards were determined to keep this strategic coast. Missionaries began their work and ultimately Father Cancer was proven right. The influence of the missions spread slowly, followed by colonists. Relations with the Indians steadily improved, but European diseases had resulted in a massive decline of the Indian population. Those remaining became dependent upon the missions, while St Augustine would not have survived but for the food grown by the mission Indians.

Meanwhile the treasure ships became the great plate fleets. In addition to Mexican and South American gold and silver, the Spanish traders would sail across the Pacific to the Far East, returning laden with silks, porcelain, and spices of immense value. From Acapulco the goods were carried overland to Vera Cruz, where the heavily armed fleets were assembled.

Piracy promised massive profits to the quick and lucky. Queen Elizabeth's Sir Francis Drake sacked and burned St Augustine in 1586. A century of war and piracy convinced Spain that a better fort was required, and the result was the Castillo de San Marcos. It withstood British sieges in 1702 and 1740, protecting the citizens when St Augustine itself was ravaged. However, the 1702 raids by Governor Moore of Carolina did end the mission system, forcing Spaniards and Christianized Indians to take refuge in St Augustine. Other Indians were pressed into the vacant territory, many of whom were members of the Creek confederacy. To the white man these Indians all looked the same, and the tag Seminole was given to them, regardless of their different languages and customs.

Although Britain was unable to take St Augustine by force, her fortunes were reversed when Havana was wrested from Spanish Control. A strategic but indefensible Florida was swapped for Havana, and the Spanish soldiers, settlers, and Christianized Indians set sail for the Caribbean. The British found themselves in control of a wilderness. Their inventory stated that St Augustine had some 500 dwellings. Pensacola had been settled and abandoned before St Augustine, and the resettled town had scarcely grown beyond the original garrison. The 400 miles between contained only San Marcos de Apalache (St Marks), which was more fort than town. Britain had great plans for Florida, but the War of Independence intervened, and the land was returned to Spain after only 20 years.

Border disputes broke out between the newly created United States and Spain, complicated by a conflict between Britain and her former colony during 1812-14. Major General Andrew Jackson led a campaign against the British throughout northern Florida. Britain withdrew from Florida, leaving behind weapons for the Seminoles and ex-slaves, who were attacked in a campaign later known as the First Seminole War. With so many incursions of American soldiers, Spain's hold upon Florida was obviously weak. In 1821 the Floridas were seceded to the United States in a treaty where the US (temporarily) relinquished any rights to Texas.

The Second Seminole War began in 1835 when, after major treaty-breaking on both sides, the US Government attempted to move all Indians to Indian territory. The chiefs were brought together and coerced to sign a new treaty, which was never ratified. Legend says that a charismatic young brave named Osceola slashed the treaty with his knife, promising *that* would be the only treaty. In the confusion several were killed, including a general and the sole chief who signed the treaty. Indian braves inspired by Osceola later ambushed Major Dade and two companies, massacring all but one of the 111 men. In the most expensive Indian war of all time, the US Army could not win against the guerilla tactics employed by the Indians. However, in 1837 Osceola, by then great leader, was imprisoned despite being under a US white flag of truce. Protests were held across America, but Osceola remained in prison until he died. He was buried in Fort Moultrie, South Carolina, minus his head. That was preserved in a jar and displayed for many years in a circus sideshow. At a final cost of $20 million and untold lives, the Seminoles were shipped to Indian territories. Those who refused to go hid in the Everglades, and under Chief Billy Bowlegs they emerged in 1855, starting the Third and final Seminole War. Billy was eventually sent west, but the United States never defeated the *entire* Seminole nation. According to some, the US Government and Seminoles are still technically at war.

Despite the 'Indian problems', Florida became a state in 1845. The strong southern influence drew a fledgling Florida into yet more conflict during the 'War Between The States', known in the north as the Civil War. Florida provided some 15,000 troops for the Confederates, and produced vital salt, pitch, and cotton for the cause. The Kissimmee Cow Hunters made Florida a major beef producer for the southern war effort. Battles took place at Olustee, where the Confederates defeated the Union Army attacking the lines of supply, and at Natural Bridge where Tallahassee, the capital, was saved.

Reconstruction did little to aid a war-torn Florida economy, but two northerners did. Henry Bradley Plant and Henry Morrison Flagler developed the west and east coasts respectively. Plant, often called the father of Tampa, came to La Florida so that his first wife could enjoy the healthy climate. Although a Connecticut Yankee, he helped the South to organize his industries during the Civil War, and later put together the 'Plant System'. His network of rails and steamships linked the Gulf Coast of Florida with the rest of America.

Plant's main competitor was Henry Flagler, who developed resorts and railroads along the Atlantic and was a partner of John D. Rockefeller at the Standard Oil Company. Flagler and his railroad moved steadily south, from St Augustine through Ormond Beach to Palm Beach. Legend says that Mrs Julia De Forest Tuttle lured Flagler to Miami. A severe frost had wiped out the orange industry as far south as Palm Beach, so she sent him some untouched blossoms from her garden. Flagler lived to see his Overseas Railway reach Key West, with steamship links to Cuba. Hundreds of construction workers died when hurricanes struck, and eventually a big one put the railroad to rest. However, the foundations were later used to complete the Key West Overseas Highway, and may still be seen today.

The Florida economy received boosts from the Spanish-American War, and the two World Wars. Many troops stationed there returned afterwards, or told friends of the healthy Florida climate. The wars brought money, but with the prosperity came problems. Black rights raised its ugly head in the mid-1950s when the Florida Supreme

*Florida has a thousand golf courses for the use of visitors and residents*

*Florida is heaven on earth for water sports enthusiasts*

Court refused to follow a US Supreme Court directive to admit a Black American to the University of Florida. Desegregation proceeded, albeit slowly, under the late Governor LeRoy Collins' effort to maintain civil order.

Meanwhile, the wars had also brought technology. Rocketry became important, first for military and later for civilian applications. Cape Canaveral was chosen as launch site for the first manned space flights by a fledgling NASA. A succession of Mercury, Gemini, and Apollo missions allowed Neil Armstrong to broadcast his message: 'The Eagle has landed' on 20 July 1969.

The arrival of Walt Disney World set the scene for unparalleled growth. Every tourist record ever made has been surpassed by Walt Disney World, whose annual visitor count exceeds the population of many countries.

## What is a Floridian?

Outsiders call any Floridian who speaks with a southern drawl a cracker, which originally applied to the whip-cracking cow hunter. Visitors should be careful when using this term, as it can mean 'poor white trash'. But apart from notable exceptions like St Augustine and Key West, Florida was settled from the north by Southerners. Their descendants may work as car mechanics or advertising executives, but they have inherited the south's hospitality. In northern and central Florida — outside the tourist belt — life moves at a slower pace.

The original Indians of Florida are long gone, wiped out by European diseases. Seminoles are the best known group found in Florida, and they have reservations outside Tampa and Fort Lauderdale, as well as in the Everglades. Having been given some of their land back, or at least income from it, the tribes are becoming increasingly businesslike. Seminole bingo and Seminole smoke shops are moneymaking additions to the old tourist related activities, such as selling Indian artifacts and wrestling alligators.

Florida's sub-tropical winters are a beacon to the snow birds — Americans and Canadians from up north — so called because they migrate with the season and come in flocks. The chill winters drive them south, from as far away as Alaska. Snow birds from New York, New England, and the eastern provinces of Canada congregate along the Atlantic Coast, while the Gulf Coast will see people from the great heartland of America and Canada. Thousands come down the highways in great motorhomes, like a procession of snails, although most buy or rent a property. Eventually they decide that there is no reason to return home each summer, and retire to Florida.

Communities are springing up everywhere, totally geared to these retired people, many of whom like to be active. Volunteer retired people are behind the highly successful programs which many Florida museums operate, and they also help innumerable other non-profit organizations.

The Spanish left Florida, but their Hispanic descendents have returned *en masse*. Miami is notorious for having zones where only Spanish is spoken, but the Cuban refugees took over and are revitalizing unwanted sections. Brazilians and others have swelled the Cuban ranks, and today their connections make important contributions to the Florida economy. Overseas banking is the financial lifeblood of Miami, and Latin American visitors come to Miami, not so much as tourists, but for marathon shopping sessions.

## Surf and Turf

Everyone expects great seafood, but Florida is also a prime beef producer. Even the produce is fresh, since most is grown locally, and the 45,000 restaurants offer unbelievable choice. Try local specialties, like Cuban sandwiches, Key lime pie, gulf shrimp, and stone crab claws. The latter are delicious hot with butter, but even better the local way — cold with mustard. Cuban and Creole restaurants can be found in Miami, Tampa, and beyond. Cajun food from New Orleans has travelled down the Panhandle to the whole of Florida, and their excellent gumbos and blackened recipes make a spicy alternative. Apart from local specialities, there are also Italian, Greek, and Chinese restaurants. The Florida highways are lined with fast-food franchises and national restaurant chains, and Americans cherish them for their value, service and reliability.

## What's on in Florida

Water sports are a great attraction in Florida for beating the heat, both on the beach and off. Snorkeling and diving are popular in the Keys, along the 1,300 miles of coastline, among the reefs, and inland in the springs. Florida is a great place to learn to dive or hone diving skills, with numerous resorts offering PADI courses. Canoe, windsurfer, hobie cat, and jet ski rentals surround the resorts, while charter boat captains know all the best fishing locations. Cruises run from hour long sightseeing on inland waterways to sailings for a week or more from Port of Miami, Everglades (Fort Lauderdale), St Petersburg/Tampa, and Canaveral.

Florida law requires tourists and residents alike to be 21 years old to purchase or drink alcohol. Beer and wine can be purchased in grocery stores, but distilled spirits are only available in 'package' liquor stores, often found in shopping plazas or as part of a bar/lounge. Opening times vary, but over-the-counter sales are prohibited on Sundays until after 1pm. Bars and lounges often offer large screen televisions or piped-in radio. Hotels large enough to have live entertainment usually have quiet lounges as well, and both are normally open to non-residents. Tiki bars have a Polynesian flavour, and the food platters and snacks are useful to help combat the potent cocktails. A growing trend in Florida, especially around the Orlando-Kissimmee area, is the dining extravaganza. Umpteen course meals are given in the party atmosphere of a Mardi Gras or an English medieval banquet, with or without jousting knights.

The theme parks are well-known crowd pleasers, but there is also considerable culture within Florida. There are fine art galleries, historical museums, and fascinating architecture — often in the same setting, surrounded by luxuriant tropical gardens. The performing arts have always been popular, with cosy backstreet theatres and new, specially-built complexes offering major national productions.

## A Florida Sampler

With so much to see and do in Florida, the main problem facing potential visitors is deciding where to go. Orlando and Walt Disney World are positioned centrally in Florida, with an incredible diversity of things to see and do. Occasional visits to the natural surroundings of a state park or beach will reduce the strain on both physique and wallet. Many holidaymakers now go for a split booking, with a week in central Florida and another on a beach. The Clearwater and St Petersburg Beaches are one of the most popular choices, with plenty of activities for all ages. The southern Gulf Coast beaches from Sarasota to Naples are also good options. Walt Disney World may be reached more quickly from Sarasota than a beach at Clearwater/St Petersburg, due to the latter's congested traffic. Pensacola to Panama City is considered Florida's finest beach by many, with the nearby capital of Tallahassee an interesting diversion.

Greater Miami comprises a cosmopolitan city, the renowned beaches, and many attractions. Miami is also within driving distance of the Everglades and the Florida Keys, but travellers should allocated days rather than hours to explore these interesting diversions. The myriad cruise options from Miami are augmented by sailings from Port Everglades and Canaveral. The resorts north of Miami each have their own character, from the exuberant wealth of Fort Lauderdale to the more reserved Palm Beach. Cocoa Beach offers all the facilities beachgoers could desire, plus easy access to the Kennedy Space Center and central Orlando. The Daytona Beach area attracts a mixture of young and old, the latter sometimes preferring quieter Ormond Beach. St Augustine has both history and beaches, while just north of Jacksonville is Florida's first resort, Amelia Island.

Perhaps a *smorgasbord* is best, a tasty mix of the areas that appeal most. A summer tour could include all or part of: Capital Tallahassee, the Gulf Coast beaches of Panhandle Florida, a trip on the Suwannee or St Johns River, historic St Augustine or Amelia Island, not forgetting their Atlantic beaches. A winter tour could incorporate: Greater Miami, the Florida Keys, the Everglades, and the Gulf or Gold Coast. Either tour is fine in spring and autumn, and numerous bargains can be found during the 'hurricane' season of autumn. The central attractions — the environs of Tampa, Orlando, Walt Disney World and Kennedy Space Center's Spaceport USA — are unsurpassed year-round. The true magic of Florida is its variety.

*Florida's marine life can be studied underwater . . .*

*. . . or on the table*

# 1

# GREATER MIAMI

Three major attractions bring over eight million visitors to Greater Miami each year. The beaches are an obvious draw, coupled with a sub-subtropical climate which allows year-round enjoyment of the wide stretches of sand. Elegant ocean liners are another inducement, with daily sailings at the Port of Miami, cruise capital of the world. But the ace up Miami's sleeve is her vibrant, cosmopolitan atmosphere. *Miami Vice* has over-dramatized the criminal aspect, but the fact remains that more than half of Miami's population are immigrants. The samba pulses through the city, tinged with jazz.

Julia Tuttle is credited with luring railroad magnate Henry Flagler to Miami. The advent of the railroad spurred millionaires, and eventually millions, to make Miami their home, which was almost named Flagler in his honour. While progress has been generally forward, Miami has had its share of hiccups. Post-war prosperity has brought a migration from city centre to suburb, leaving gaps to be filled by Cuban refugees. Many others have since followed, including Haitians and Puerto Ricans. 'Upstarts' have competed unfairly for jobs by working for below-minimum wages, causing friction between the Hispanics and Blacks, and trouble has erupted as recently as 1980.

Fortunately the success of the Cubans has shown troubled communities a way forward. The regeneration of 'Little Havana' was the result of sheer hard work by the industrious Cubans, and has been followed by 'Little Haiti'. Other indicators of Miami's growing prosperity are the skyscrapers built by financial and commercial corporations eager to tap into the Latin American connection. Perhaps money is seeping north from wealthy Coral Gables and trendy Coconut Grove, gradually rebuilding Miami from the south. Downtown Miami is still undergoing its beauty treatment, so one may still find relics of old Miami nestled among the towers of glass and steel.

# Getting Around Miami

Miami streets are based upon a grid pattern, and are divided into four (unequal) quadrants by Flagler Street and Miami Avenue. Throughout most of Miami the streets run East-West and avenues North-South, and both are numbered sequentially. Thus 1050 Southwest 8th Street is eight streets south of Flagler Street. The street or avenue number may be divided by 100 to find out how many blocks from Flagler Street or Miami Avenue one is. Therefore 1050 Southwest 8th Street is 10.5 blocks west of Miami Avenue, between 10th and 11th Avenues. Southwest 8th Street is, by the way, better known as Calle Ocho, the heart of Little Havana.

Miami International Airport is well served by domestic and international flights, with connections to the Caribbean, Central and South America. Many hotels have free hotlines at the airport, and the nearer ones offer a free shuttle service. For Miami Beach, Fort Lauderdale, and Palm Beach hotels, the Super Shuttle is less expensive than taxi or limousine. Lightly burdened travellers may also take the Metrobus from the airport to Central Miami, but luggage security and finding the right connections can be a hassle.

In addition to national ground-based passenger networks, such as Amtrak Rail and Greyhound-Trailways Bus, Dade County has its own public transportation system. Metrorail runs from Hialeah in the north through downtown Miami to Kendall in the south. The Metrobus network is almost too extensive, and the individual timetables and routemaps fill a small suitcase. An overall map is available which, when supplemented with selected routes, make travelling by bus easier. Yet another option is Tri-Rail between Miami, Fort Lauderdale, and West Palm Beach. They have a very handy bus feeder network on weekdays (free) and weekends (charges may apply), which include most holiday attractions. Since it is primarily a rail network for linking the three cities, it is no use for travelling from one part of Miami to another, but it is useful for travel to Fort Lauderdale or Palm Beach. The converse is also true, and when staying 'up north' at Palm Beach or Fort Lauderdale one may take Tri-Rail down to Miami Metrozoo, Vizcaya, and Bayside Marketplace, to name but a few. They also provide connections between airports in the three counties, and links to Metrorail and Metrobus.

Metromover is in downtown Miami. This totally automated people mover circles above the downtown area every few minutes. Metromover travels between the major blocks of offices, and also provides long-distant connections via the Metrorail and Metrobus networks.

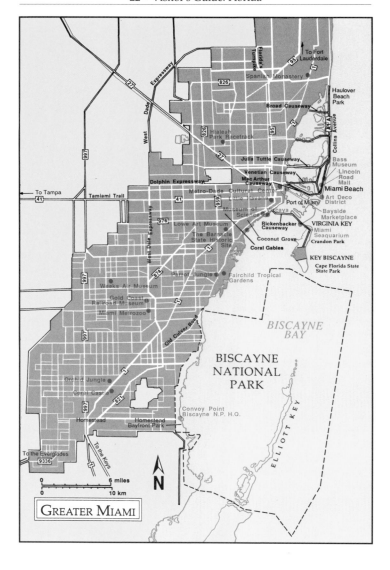

GREATER MIAMI

*Bayside Marketplace by night*

*Dolphins entertain visitors to the Miami Seaquarium*

# Central Miami

The most obvious and accessible downtown Miami parking is on US Highway 1 (Biscayne Boulevard, East of NE 2nd Ave) adjacent to **Bayside Marketplace**. This latest addition to Miami combines a public park with a modern shopping and dining complex overlooking Biscayne Bay. The shops and surroundings border on trendy and the walkways are frequented by street performers, giving a carnival atmosphere. In the evenings the bars and restaurants overlooking the central courtyard, marina, and bay are popular, and the marketplace is well known for its quality free entertainment. Sightseeing boats at the marina give daytime and sunset tours of Biscayne Bay.

Bayside Marketplace is also a good base for exploring Miami by land. The Metromover can be caught a block or so west of the Marketplace, and taken for the quick circle above downtown Miami. Near the Metrorail and Metrobus Terminus is the **Metro-Dade Cultural Center**, home to the Dade County Main Library and two museums of note. The scope of the **Historical Museum of South Florida** goes beyond that implied in the name. Their three-dimensional walk-through history includes all of Florida, highlighting its different cultures. Of course, Southern Florida is not neglected. There are interesting subjects, like the lifestyle of the Seminole Indians or wrecking in Key West. The cultural diversity of Miami is well presented, and the history walk takes visitors from paleo-Indian times right up to the present. In addition to permanent exhibits there are topical or tropical diversions, which change regularly.

It is impossible to predict what will be on show at the **Museum of Fine Arts** — everything is subject to change. Anything can and often is rearranged to best display the many travelling exhibitions they hold each year. Reduced admission is available on combined Arts Center and Historical Museum tickets.

The terracotta facing and wrought-iron detail of the **Gusman Center** hides a performing arts complex with an interior resembling an Italian courtyard. The Philharmonic Orchestra of Florida, the younger New World Symphony, the Miami City Ballet and Miami Film Festival perform here. Opera fans can catch the Greater Miami Opera at the Dade County Auditorium on 2901 W Flagler.

As an introduction to Miami, the Old Town Trolley is almost indispensable. Interspersed with the colourful history are interesting glimpses into life within the differing communities which comprise Miami. From Bayside Marketplace the trolley will stop at selected destinations, such as Vizcaya, Coconut Grove, and Coral Gables, and pass through Little Havana and the downtown area.

Passengers may disembark at any stop, rejoining a later trolley, which pass every half hour. The trolley tour may be commenced at any stop, treating Bayside Marketplace as just another destination. Seaquarium or Vizcaya, with free parking, make popular starting points. The trip is useful for delving further into Miami, just for the sheer fun of it. The route is comprehensive, so for convenience this guide will use a similar order. The trolley does not stop in Little Havana nor does it reach Key Biscayne, but the narration will.

South from Bayside Marketplace is a row of tall condominiums and office buildings lining Biscayne Bay. This area was known as Millionaire's Row, after the well-to-do who made bayside Miami their winter residence. The south-eastern quadrant of Miami is the smallest, and their diagonal roads are the main exception to the rule of streets running east-west and avenues north-south.

The Rickenbacker Causeway can get busy on a hot weekend, which is most of the year. Sun seekers grab patches of sand from the first narrow strip along the causeway all around Virginia Key and **Key Biscayne**. The best beaches are on the latter, while **Miami Seaquarium** is on Virginia Key. The trolley stops there before returning to the mainland. Behind the main entrance is the original seaquarium, with two storeys of viewing ports into the water and a stadium above for the dolphin show. Lolita, star of the Killer Whale Show, is at the newer seaquarium on the left. Dolphins get top billing again at the Flipper Show. In between the main shows there are shark and sea lion feeding exhibitions and the Manatees. A visit may be rounded off with the aquariums, touch pools, a simulated rain forest, and a full selection of gift shops and food emporiums.

Sailboats and jet ski rentals may be found along the causeway leading to Virginia Key, and a marina is located further out at Key Biscayne. Beyond that is Crandon Park, operated by Dade County, with about every facility a park could conceivably contain, including the Key Biscayne Golf Course. Parking is on a first come basis, and the beach and picnic areas are especially popular on weekends.

For a slightly quieter park try **Bill Baggs Cape Florida State Recreation Area**, on the southern tip of Key Biscayne, with picnicking and just over a mile of beach. The energetic can walk the two-mile loop or the shorter nature trail. Except for Tuesdays the park offers tours of the lighthouse, which is the oldest remaining structure in South Florida, despite attacks by Seminoles and Confederate troops.

**Vizcaya**, on the mainland overlooking Biscayne Bay, was the grand winter home of the late James Deering, co-founder and vice president of International Harvester. Like many rich industrialists, he travelled extensively through Europe and accumulated a great wealth of sculpture, textiles, furniture, and ornamental extras, spanning some 400 years. Vizcaya was conceived as a sixteenth-century Italian Renaissance villa which had been extended and modernized through the ages. When Vizcaya was completed in 1916 it looked four centuries old, and the formal gardens were the final touch. Modern day visitors see Vizcaya much as Deering left it, including furnishings and art. Several hours should be allowed for even a casual examination of the thirty-four rooms open to the public and the extensive gardens, part formal and part original hardwood.

A large village was required to support the Deering estate, and its remains are across the road. Situated there is the **Miami Museum of Science & Space Transit Planetarium**, with hands-on experiments in science, nature, health, and the environment. Good use is made of computer technology, while many of the learning experiences for the younger children are based on comic book heros.

**Coconut Grove** was annexed by Miami in 1925, but the Grove has fiercely retained its identity and a relaxed, almost continental charm. The Grove can be found in southwest Miami, and is centred where Bay Shore Drive and Main Highway meet Grand Avenue. The

*The lighthouse at Bill Baggs State Park is the oldest surviving building in southern Florida*

trolley stops outside Mayfair in the Grove, an upmarket shopping complex which fills several city blocks with fountains, tropical greenery, restaurants, neatly hidden shops, and a hotel. A new competitor of theirs is the CocoWalk, with a less enclosed shopping area, restaurants, and an eight-screen cinema. Alfresco dining is the order of the day in the bohemian atmosphere of the Grove, especially around Commodore Plaza, where sharply dressed executives conduct their business, and well heeled tourists model the latest in resort fashions. Coconut Grove is just as pleasant and perhaps a bit cooler in the evening, and many Miamians go there for the nightlife.

Check the Coconut Grove Playhouse, just south of Commodore Plaza, for current productions. They have won national acclaim for the quality of their performances and the stars they attract. Park at the playhouse by day for a step back to the earliest days of Coconut Grove at **The Barnacle**. This state historic site was home to Commodore Ralph Munroe, noted shipwright, wrecker, and photographer. The bustle of the Grove dissolves immediately upon entering the hardwood forest leading to the house, which is just as the commodore left it. The number of personal artifacts is a pleasant touch, and

*Dine alfresco at elegant Coconut Grove*

*A quarry in Coral Gables became the Venetian Pool*

his many photographs recreate the earliest days of the grove. The simple style of the house and grounds make an interesting contrast with the Gothic atmosphere of Vizcaya. The trolley will head inland, but drivers may prefer to continue south towards the Old Cutler Road using the directions in the Greater Miami section.

A sharp contrast also exists between the relaxed, older Coconut Grove and **Coral Gables**, due west of the Grove. Coral Gables was planned, down to the colour of the sidewalks, by George Merrick when he turned his 1,600 acres of hammock and swamp into some of the world's most valuable property in the land boom of the early 1920s. Wealthy people were attracted to the orderly atmosphere of a planned development. Property values continue to rocket, and the tree-lined avenues offer some of the safest driving and cycling around Miami.

The trolley includes much of Coral Gables, giving fascinating insights into the codes and restrictions that preserve their unique atmosphere. Unfortunately it does not include the **Lowe Art Mu-**  **seum**, but non-drivers may get there by Metrorail, taking the University of Miami exit. Lowe's collection includes Renaissance and Baroque, Early American, American Indian, pre-Columbian, and Asian. One of their more recent additions, *The Football Player* by renowned modern sculptor Duane Hanson, is such a realistic portrayal that a sign was erected to stop the public from pinching him.

North of the University area are golf courses (two public, one private) and Coral Gables' most imposing structure, the Biltmore Hotel. Another example of the lifestyle of the 1920s is the **Venetian Pool**. Built where coral rock was quarried for constructing homes in Coral Gables, it must rank as one of the most opulent public swimming baths in the world. The massive baths offers a few modern touches as well: the 800,000 gallons of water are recycled through the Florida aquifer, important in water conscious Miami, and a wheelchair elevator provides access for the handicapped to the pool. Having paid the admission fee, ask them to turn on the waterfall.

The main shopping area in Coral Gables is along the Miracle Mile, which joins up with SW 22nd Street in Miami. Many of the shops are very smart, but may appear old fashioned to younger generations brought up in the ubiquitous shopping mall. If the summer heat gets too bad, dip into the cool marble surroundings of the Collonade Hotel (the trolley stops here) and its air-conditioned shops. The Mediterranean-style City Hall is nearby, as is the Greyhound Bus Station. When leaving Coral Gables look out for their famous stone arches, which herald the borders of their domain.

One road with four names marks the northern boundary of Coral

Gables. The Tamiami Trail (US Highway 41) links Tampa to Miami, and the latter section is SW 8th Street, better known locally as Calle Ocho. The Cuban influence is increasingly noticeable as Calle Ocho becomes one-way on approaching Miami, in the heart of **Little Havana.** Although it cannot boast the wealth of Coconut Grove or Coral Gables, Little Havana is a success story, where industrious Cuban refugees have wrested a living out of the jungle which inner Miami had become. People visit the Cuban community surrounding Calle Ocho because it is like visiting a foreign country without leaving Miami. One whole week in March is dedicated to celebrating the Hispanic heritage with numerous events. A movement is afoot to continue developing the area, changing the name to the Latin Quarter, reflecting other residents such as Portuguese and Brazilians. Sample this blending of Hispanic culture with American overtones by trying a *medianoche* at one of the many places to eat along Calle Ocho. Those willing to go off the beaten path a bit may enjoy the excellent food and busy atmosphere at La Esquina de Tejas (101 SW 12th Avenue) or the Latin American Cafeteria on 2940 SW 22nd.

The trolley drives through Little Havana, but to savour it properly one must walk its streets. The shops primarily cater for the locals, and entering a grocery store is harking back to the days before convenience foods. Some of the best bread in America is found there, the secret ingredient in the Cuban Sandwich. Much of the local life can be seen in the streets and shops, and at El Credito one can buy hand-rolled cigars. Those who enjoy spectator sports should head for the 'exclusive' men-only Domino Park. No one under 55 years old is admitted, but the click of the tiles can be heard a block away. 'Youngsters' must watch from a distance because the matches are treated seriously, as are the heated discussions on politics.

The trolley drives through the downtown Miami shopping district, which is currently undergoing rejuvenation, before returning to Bayside Marketplace.

## Miami Beach

Miami Beach is more than a mere wide stretch of sand between Miami and the Atlantic Ocean. It is a city and an island unto itself. From bayside Miami the beach is a two mile swim, so travellers who want sand within walking distance should book hotels on or near to Bayshore Drive or Collins Avenue at Miami Beach.

Sunseekers can stay in a living museum at southern Miami Beach. The **Art Deco National Historic District** is probably the world's  largest collection of these pastel buildings with rounded shapes. Many of these 1930s era edifices are beachfront hotels. The Art Deco district has since undergone considerable renovation, and has been rediscovered as a haven from the plastic 'could be anywhere' resorts. The Miami Design Preservation League provide Saturday morning walking tours of the district at 10.30am, and their welcome center on Washington Avenue also sells Art Deco artifacts.

Some of the Art Deco hotels have been converted into residences, and young, arty types are breathing life back into Miami Beach. The pedestrian-only shopping precinct of Lincoln Road is home to the South Florida Art Center, with works by local artists. Antique and art shops on Lincoln Road rub shoulders with street corner drug stores right out of the American 1960s. Sun tan lotion, T-shirts, and post-cards can also be bought on Lincoln Road, which divides Miami Beach in two between 16th and 17th Streets. Washington Avenue with a variety of shops runs two blocks behind Ocean Drive along southern Miami Beach.

The **Bass Museum of Art** has a collection which includes the works of European, American, and Asian Masters. Their changing exhibit area often reflects local Miami Beach communities, and one of these, the Jews, have erected the Holocaust Memorial on Meridian Avenue. Strollers are sometimes startled by the massive 42-ft bronze arm, reaching skyward with life-sized figures clinging to it.

Travelling north up Miami Beach the buildings get progressively higher, but never *quite* so high as imagination or postcards portray. The Miami Beach Convention Center is just north of Lincoln Road, and south of the Bass Museum of Art. Parking becomes suddenly impossible when a big exhibition like the International Boat Show is on in February, but otherwise the parking lots are handy for Lincoln Road shopping and within walking distance of the beach.

Ocean Drive ends around 15th street, but Collins Avenue proceeds north past the high rise hotels and condominiums. A mural more than 100ft high marks the **Fountainebleau Hilton**, one of the premier Hilton Hotels and the jewel of Miami Beach. Non-residents are welcome, and the choice of dining and entertainment is excellent. While the award-winning Dining Galleries require men to wear jacket and tie, and the Club Tropigala a jacket, informal wear is fine in the other five restaurants. The Tropigala offers evening entertainment with Las Vegas and Latin revues, two orchestras, and fine continental dining. Several lounges have live entertainment nightly, and if the daytime heat gets unbearable, cool down with a non-alcoholic daiquiri in the Garden Lobby Bar.

Some of the best up-market shopping is available at 9700 Collins Avenue in Bal Harbour. Across the bridge from there is Haulover Beach Park with a fishing pier, plenty of beach access, and a marina

*The Fountainebleau Hilton is the jewel in Miami Beach's crown*

*Orchid Jungle, where native and exotic species thrive in the sub-tropical climate of southern Florida*

with sightseeing boats. Over the Intracoastal Waterway on the mainland is the popular Oleta State Park, with canoeing up the Oleta River, picnicking and pleasant walks.

## Greater Miami Environs

The metropolis of Miami extents towards Fort Lauderdale, west into the Everglades, and south towards the Keys. Within the commuter belt of Miami are some of the region's most interesting diversions.

Northeast of Miami is the **Church of St Bernard de Clairvaux**, also known as the Ancient Spanish Monastery. This magnificent stone chapel and cloisters was constructed in the Province of Segovia, Spain, in 1133-41, predating Miami by some 750 years. William Randolph Hearst, collector extraordinaire, purchased the cloisters for his never to be completed Californian Castle, but the monastery was impounded at the east coast. The US Department of Agriculture confiscated the packing crates after an outbreak of foot and mouth disease in Spain, and the mixed-up stones became the world's largest puzzle. Today the restored monastery is a house of worship for the Episcopal Diocese of South Florida. The early Gothic cloisters are open daily, as is the gift shop and surrounding grounds.

Also in the northeast is the **American Police Hall of Fame and Museum**. This houses a large collection of real and fictional police vehicles (like the car from the film *Blade Runner*), and a memorial to officers who have fallen in the line of duty. Visitors are invited to solve crimes, examine the devices used by police and criminals, and perhaps spend some time in jail.

One of the most pleasant drives around the Miami environs is to the southwest. The first part is Bay Shore Drive to Coconut Grove, along the Old Town Trolley route. The following route will put the driver onto Old Cutler Road. From Bayshore Drive bear right on Grand Avenue and almost immediately left onto Main Highway. Fork left onto Douglas Street then right onto Ingraham Highway and left at Le Jeune Road. Across the canal is a rare sight in America, a traffic roundabout, beyond which is Old Cutler Road. This route, easier than it sounds, goes through the nicest areas of Coconut Grove and past the new bayside developments of Coral Grove.

An older Miami borders the Old Cutler Road south, with streets lined by live oak or imported banyan. On the left is **Matheson Hammock Park**, one of the largest in Miami, with picnic areas, beach, a marina, a pool, and good birdwatching. The entrance to **Fairchild Tropical Gardens** is just beyond Matheson, and alone is worth the drive. With 83 acres and 5,000 species of plants, this is the largest tropical botanical garden in America. To preserve the tranquil atmosphere picnicking, musical instruments, loud radios, and playing games are prohibited. Regular guided tram tours of the park give an introduction to the garden.

When Old Cutler Road reaches Red Road, one may detour north for **Parrot Jungle**. This Miami tourist landmark for over 50 years is the largest and slickest of the commercial enterprises in Florida that assume tropical foliage looks better when decorated with colourful birds. Native and exotic plants and birds are on display, and feeding the animals is positively encouraged.

The estate of Charles Deering is hidden one block east of the Old Cutler Road on SW 168th street. Less flamboyant than James Deering, who built Vizcaya, Charles' home and grounds are not so pretentious. There are good views of Biscayne Bay and, being off the main tourist routes, is another spot for quiet contemplation.

The Old Cutler Road eventually reaches US Highway 1, which stretches from Key West in Florida to the Canadian Border of Maine. One man's labour of love may be seen at **Coral Castle**, which was built entirely of local coral rock. The structure is impressive, although the mystery surrounding it appears to be slightly exaggerated. **Orchid Jungle** is due north of Coral Castle on Norton Road, where beautiful orchids grow in the sub-tropical climate. Their plant shop may be visited free.

Due south on Newton, and then east on North Canal Road is **Biscayne National Underwater Park**. Despite its name, the park preserves considerable shore line and several islands south of Miami, and the visitor centre and tour offices at Convoy Point are on dry land. The underwater sections of the park can be explored in the morning by glassbottom boat, or by snorkeling or diving among some of Florida's finest coral reefs in the afternoon. During the winter/spring peak season there is often an extra boat tour in the afternoon, especially on weekends, given sufficient demand.

The snorkeling trips are geared for families, with excellent snorkeling equipment supplied. Divers are also welcome, unless they have picked up the bad habits of touching and standing on the fragile coral. The park concessionaire also runs a gift shop, rents canoes, and is very active in conserving the Florida Keys. The visitor center has interpretive exhibits, and a naturalist narrates the glassbottom boat tours, which include viewing coral reefs, sponge beds and protected islands (without landing on them). Calling ahead to pre-book tours and special activities is advisable. To reach the local Keys one needs a private boat or enough people to charter a glassbottom boat. The islands offer overnight camping, interpretive centres, and a place to play *Robinson Crusoe*.

The **Miami Metrozoo** is south of Miami on SW 152nd Street, west of US Highway 1 and the Florida Turnpike. Their cageless, near-natural habitats for the animals and mission to preserve endangered animals makes them a leader in 'state-of-the-zoo'. Disabled facilities are good, and an air-conditioned monorail provides an introductory overview of the zoo. In general the animals are grouped by continent and habitat, and many co-exist as they would in the wild. The Metrozoo makes excellent use of trained people to answer questions or help spot the animals which, due to the cageless design, may have retired to a quiet or sheltered site. The pictographs give instant verification of the habitat, diet, period of activity, and endangered status of the many species. Firm favourite is the white tiger enclosure, which resembles a Buddhist temple, and the Wings of Asia, a $1^1/_2$ acre free-flight aviary. Even a cursory walk through the aviary will reveal many vividly coloured inhabitants, but check for feeding time at the entrance, when even the most elusive birds can be seen. Spread over 290 acres, Metrozoo includes gift shops, two theatres, classrooms, restaurants and snacks, and a special petting and education facility for children.

Two other attractions exist near the Metrozoo, the first being next door. The **Gold Coast Railroad Museum** has an armoured Presidential Rail Car, exhibits highlighting the history of Henry Flagler's East Coast Railroad, and enough equipment to go into competition with Amtrak. The New Tamiami Airport may be found by taking SW 152nd Street, the Metrozoo road, further west and then heading north on Lindgren Road. **Weeks Air Museum** is in the airport, and has aircraft from the early era of flight to World War II. Many of their pristine aircraft are maintained in flying condition, and they also have a less publicized collection of prize-winning aerobatic monoplanes and biplanes.

Betting sports enthusiasts are well catered for in Greater Miami. Biscayne, Flagler, and Hollywood are all greyhound tracks, and horses run at Calder Race Course and Gulfstream Park. Jai-Alai, pronounced Hi-Aleye, is a ball game where the furious pace of the betting is only exceeded by the speed of play.

# Cruising from Miami

Cruises of Biscayne Bay or Fort Lauderdale can be arranged at Bayside Marketplace or the Miami Beach Marina, but for a 'real' cruise ship, head for the **Port of Miami**. Star boats include Royal Caribbean Cruise Line's *Nordic Empress* and *Sovereign of the Seas*, and Carnival Cruise Lines' *Fantasy* and *Ecstasy*. Fort Lauderdale's Port Everglades is also just around the bend, with a good complement of cruise ships. *SeaEscape* and *Discovery* have day cruises to the Bahamas or day and half-day cruise experiences to 'nowhere'. Cruises from Miami can be booked from virtually anywhere in the world, with or without flights, and innumerable travel agents in Miami will make bookings for those who suddenly fancy a day or more of their vacation on the high seas.

Passengers on cruises which dock at a foreign port must have their passports, which are necessary to get back into America even if you remain shipboard. Remember to allow time to see Miami if booking a cruise.

## *Additional Information*

### *Visitor Information*
Greater Miami Convention &
    Visitors Bureau
701 Brickell Avenue, Suite 2700
Miami FL 33131
☎ 305-539-3000 (FAX 305-539-3113)

### *Local Events*

*Jan 1*
Orange Bowl Football Classic
Orange Bowl Stadium, Miami

*Mid Jan*
Art Deco Weekend Festival
Ocean Drive, South Miami Beach

Beaux Arts Festival
University of Miami Campus
Coral Gables

Taste of the Grove
Peacock Park, Coconut Grove

*Early Feb*
Miami Film Festival
Miami Beach Convention Center

*Mid Feb*
Coconut Grove Arts Festival
Coconut Grove

Miami International Boat Show
Miami Beach Convention Center

*Early March*
Carnival Miami
& Calle Ocho Festival
Orange Bowl Stadium
& Calle Ocho, Miami

*Mid to End March*
Lipton International Tennis Players
    Championship
International Tennis Center,
Key Biscayne

*Early April*
Coconut Grove Musical Festival
Peacock Park

*Mid April*
Coconut Grove Seafood Festival
Peacock Park

*4 July*
July 4th at Bayside
Bayside Marketplace, Miami

*Early Oct*
West Indian American Miami
    Carnival Extravaganza
Miami Beach

*Early Nov*
The Miami Air Show
Opa-locka Airport

*Early Dec*
Greater Miami Boat Parade
Intracoastal Waterway

## Places of Interest

**Coconut Grove**
*The Barnacle State Historic Site*
3485 Main Hwy
FL 33133
☎ 305-448-9445
Open: 8am-sunset, tours at
10.30am, 1pm & 2.30pm
Free, tours extra
Hammock, tour, picnic, scenic, &

**Coral Gables**
*Fairchild Tropical Gardens*
10901 Old Cutler Road
FL 33156
☎ 306-667-1651
Open: 9.30am-4.30pm
Tram tours, &

*Lowe Art Museum, University of
Miami*
1301 Stanford Dr
FL 33124-6310
☎ 305-284-3536
Open: 10am-5pm Tue-Sat,
noon-5pm Sun
Kress collection, gifts, &

*Venetian Pool*
2701 DeSoto Blvd
FL 33134
☎ 305-460-5356
Opening hours vary
Pool, snack bar, & swim

**Homestead**
*Biscayne National Underwater Park*
North Canal Road
FL 33030
☎ 305-247-2400
Open: 8am-6pm, telephone for tour
times
Free for park, tours extra
Tour boat, canoe rental, swim,
snorkeling, &

*Orchid Jungle*
26715 SW 157th Ave
FL 33031
☎ 305-247-4824

Open: 8.30am-5.30pm except
Thanksgiving & Xmas
Orchid shop

**Key Biscayne**
*Cape Florida State Recreation Area*
1200 S Crandon Blvd
FL 33149
☎ 305-361-5811
Open: 8am-sunset, tours 10.30am,
1pm, 2.30pm, and 3.30pm except
Tue
Beach, picnic, lighthouse, &

**Miami**
*Bayside Marketplace*
401 Biscayne Blvd, Suite R-106
FL 33015
☎ 305-577-3344
Open: 11am-10pm, Sat 10am-10pm.
Sun 10am-8pm. Free
Marina, restaurants, shops, cafes,
boutiques, &

*Center for the Fine Arts*
101 W Flagler St
(Metro-Dade Culture Center)
FL 33130
☎ 305-375-1700
Open: 10am-5pm Tue-Sat,
noon-5pm Sun
Gifts, tours, &

*Historical Museum of South Florida*
101 West Flagler St
FL 33130
☎ 305-375-1492
Open: 10am-5pm Mon-Sat,
noon-5pm Sun
Gifts, &

*Miami Metrozoo*
12400 SW 152nd St
FL 33177
☎ 305-251-0400
Open: 9.30am-5.30pm, no entrance
after 4pm
Gifts, restaurant, docent tours, &

*Miami Museum of Science & Space
    Transit Planetarium*
3280 South Miami Ave
FL 33129
☎ 305-854-4247
Open: 10am-6pm except Thanksgiving & Xmas
Planetarium, hands-on and natural
science, gifts

*Miami Seaquarium*
4400 Rickenbacker Causeway
FL 33149
☎ 305-361-5705
Open: 9.30am-5pm, grounds close
at 6.30pm
Gifts, restaurant, ♿

*Parrot Jungle*
11000 SW 57th Ave
FL 33156
305-666-7834
9:30am-6pm, last entrance 5pm
Restaurants & snacks, gifts, ♿

*Vizcaya Museum and Gardens*
3251 S Miami Ave.
FL 33129
☎ 305-579-2813
Open: 9.30-4.30pm, except Xmas
SG tours, gifts, ♿ ground floor

*Weeks Air Museum*
14710 SW 128th St
FL 33186
☎ 305-233-5197
Open: 10am-5pm
Tours by arrangement, ♿

## Miami Beach
*Ancient Spanish Monastery*
16711 W Dixie Highway
N Miami Beach FL 33160
305-945-1461
Open: 10am-5pm Mon-Sat,
noon-5pm Sun
Chapel, cloisters, gifts, ♿

*Bass Museum of Art*
2121 Park Ave
FL 33139
☎ 305-673-7530
Open: 10am-5pm Tue-Sat,
1pm-5pm Sun
Gifts, tours by request, ♿

*Miami Design Preservation League
    (Art Deco Welcome Center)*
661 Washington Avenue
(Mail via PO Bin L)
FL 33119
☎ 305-672-2014
Opening hours vary, free
Art Deco Tour, gifts

## North Miami
*Oleta River State Recreational Area*
3400 NE 163rd Street
FL 33160
☎ 305-947-6357
Open: 8am-sunset
Beach, picnic, canoe, swim, bike
trail, ♿

## *Tours and Transport*

## Miami
*Old Town Trolley*
From Bayside Marketplace
FL 33101
☎ 305-374-8687
Open: 9am-4.30pm
Guided tour, off-on privileges

*SeaEscape*
1080 Port Blvd
FL 33132
☎ 305-379-0000
Departures vary
Meals, entertainment, casino, ♿

# 2

# THE FLORIDA KEYS

The Keys are a feast. For starters is an impossibly colourful sea laced with live coral and sporting a rainbow of fish. For salad the tropical extravaganza includes the choicest mangroves and finest South American hardwoods, topped with Heart of Palm. For beaches the Keys can dredge up a soupçon of sand, and they usually have to. For a hearty steak try Key Largo, and for the fish course perhaps the excellent seafood of Islamorada and Marathon. Their world famous dessert is, of course, the Key Lime Pie at Key West.

## Introducing The Keys

The Keys, and there are about a hundred of them, are comprised of ancient coral surrounded by salt-tolerant mangroves, with hardwood, palm, and pine centers. The word Key comes from *Cayo* or 'little island'. Although any Florida isle may be called a key, in plural form it refers only to the Florida Keys, which stretch beyond Key West to the Dry Tortugas. The forty-two bridges of the Overseas Highway link most of the inhabited Keys, commencing with Key Largo, the largest, and ending at Key West.

First time arrivals at the Keys learn the reason for the jest, 'a soupçon of sand'. The living coral reefs which surround the Keys block the sand producing waves which would otherwise roll in from the Atlantic. Apart from Bahia Honda, where the beaches are naturally created by a gap in the reef, they are mostly man-made.

Yet it is water sports which draw the visitors, with some of the best diving and snorkeling in North America. Fantastically coloured fish dart amongst the exotic coral shapes and half-buried wrecks. Glassbottom boats cater for spectators, while even confirmed landlubbers can encounter living coral in the safety of the aquarium.

Between and beyond the reefs are other opportunities for water sports, such as fishing. For newcomers unfamiliar with the reefs,

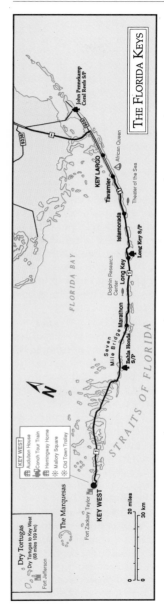

which have claimed more Spanish gold than any pirates, a tour or piloted boat may be preferable to renting one. Boats may be chartered for fishing, snorkeling, diving, sailing, or just plain messing around in.

## Towards the Keys

To the south of Miami, beyond the outskirts of Homestead and Florida City, the ubiquitous US Highway 1 undergoes a metamorphosis: filling stations, roadside motels, even billboards disappear. The flat, grassy prairies and mangrove surrounded waterways belong to the Everglades. Indeed, just before Key Largo, US 1 skirts the National Park boundary.

Once across to Key Largo, fast-food franchises, gas stations, and shopping plazas reappear. Since the only US Highway throughout the Keys is number 1, navigating is simple. Little green signs line the roadside, the milemarkers which count from 107 down to 0 in Key West. Given the distance from Key West, one only needs to know whether the attraction is bayside (right while travelling down the Keys) or oceanside. Milemarker (MM) 100.5 oceanside is left of Highway 1 when travelling towards Key West, and the fraction is a helpful indicator of how far *before* the milemarker to look.

Unfortunately, many holidaymakers consider the milemarkers a challenge — racing against time. Too many visitors head straight to Key West, but to truly experience the Keys stop occasionally and leave your car. Relax, slow the pace, and enjoy each Key in turn.

# Key Largo

The Key Largo Chamber of Commerce welcome center at MM 103.4 is a useful port of call. Located bayside in a tropical pink shopping plaza, they provide maps and information on the Keys' attractions and accommodation. Probably the most unusual is across the road at the Key Largo Undersea Park. Swimmers and snorkelers are welcome to enjoy the park, while certified divers may stay at the Jules Undersea Hotel, 5 fathoms below the surface.

At MM 102.5 is Key Largo's main attraction, **John Pennekamp Coral Reef State Park**. This busy park caters for a wide range of visitors, from laid-back sunbathers to certified divers anxious to experience real reef. Activities included with the nominal entrance fee are swimming, picknicking, walking the inland and mangrove nature trails, and an interpretive center complete with aquarium. The Park Concession runs the gamut of water-based activities, with canoes and windsurfers available for local excursions. The best coral is actually several miles beyond the park waters within the Key Largo National Marine Sanctuary, but the John Pennekamp tour boats go there anyway. All the waters surrounding the Keys are now a National Marine Sanctuary, but the older Key Largo National Marine Sanctuary has some exceptional reefs, and these are visited by the park's optional, but not to be missed, excursions.

The narration during the glassbottom boat tours is provided by a trained spotter, who identifies the species which inhabit the reef and provides a colourful introduction to the coral environment. Although there can be no guarantee of spotting any particular creature, keep an eagle eye out for sharks, dolphins, and sea turtles.

Snorkeling is an ideal way for swimmers to experience the reef at close quarters. Lessons and equipment are provided for beginners, while experienced snorkelers prefer their own gear. Water temperatures in the Keys run from the mid-70s to high 80s Fahrenheit (approximately 22-32 °C), pleasant indeed, although a short-sleeved wetsuit may be advisable in winter. Visibility is often excellent and the snorkeling reefs are not deep. Remember not to stand on or otherwise molest the coral, which is damaged by human contact.

Only certified divers are catered for at the dive shop; remember to bring that slip of paper. Reeftix, a company closely associated with the park concessionaires, are located before John Pennekamp Park. They provide a four-day certification course and a one-day introductory 'Resort' dive. The same is true of many other dive shops, which are not excluded from the park.

John Pennekamp Park also rents sailboats and powerboats, as well as providing a marina and selling bait to fisherman. Rentals and tours do depend upon weather conditions: on days of poor visibility trips are cancelled, while on ideal days they sell out fast. The park is often busy, but Easter Spring Break, when college students descend upon Florida, is particularly crazy — arrive early or not at all.

At Key Largo the *African Queen* is berthed in the marina outside the Holiday Inn at MM 100. This cute little iron-sided steamer once carried tourists and big game hunters across the waters of Africa under the name *Livingstone*. The *African Queen* became the ship's name when she co-starred with Humphrey Bogart and Katherin Hepburn in the classic film directed by John Huston. The boiler and steam engine, removed during filming and subsequently 'misplaced', were replaced by a hand-crafted reproduction in Britain. The *African Queen* was amongst ships reviewed by Her Majesty, the Queen Mother, during her 90th birthday. Today the *African Queen* can take up her original occupation of transporting tourists. (To avoid disappointment remember that the boat is often away doing charity work, and that she is not fired-up every day.)

The marina also plays host to the *Key Largo Princess*, a large glass bottom boat which also visits the coral reefs of Key Largo National Marine Sanctuary. It is not necessary to pay the entrance fee to the John Pennekamp Park to take their tour. Numerous charter boats provide half-day and full-day fishing or snorkeling trips from the Holiday Inn Marina, while others leave from the adjacent Marina del Mar. Sailing enthusiasts can find the 51.5ft *Witt's End* there, an Irwin Ketch Cutter which regularly plies the Key's chromatic waterways. The Witts run relaxing, hassle-free snorkel, sightseeing, and sunset trips on their enviable sailboat.

More seafood restaurants, marinas, and resorts lie along Highway 1, including a 200-bed Sheraton bayside resort which combines the three. Anyone not staying there can still find a beach on Key Largo at the Harry Harris County Park, MM 92.5 on the oceanside. Apart from their man-made beach, there is a salt water swimming pool and other facilities such as a softball diamond.

## Islamorada Area

Newcomers to the Keys give themselves away when they say 'Izlamorada' rather than the proper '*Eye*lamorada'. The islands from Plantation Key to Long Key are punctuated by the resorts and Tiki Bars of the self styled 'Purple Isles' centered around Islamorada. The **Theater of the Sea** on MM 84.5 bayside, with one of the best gift shops along Highway 1, provides an entertaining and educational look at marine animals. Guests are escorted from the dolphin show to the sea lion experience and then on to an alligator and turtle

*Divers at the John Pennekamp Coral Reef State Park find the unexpected sharing the reef with the multicoloured fish*

*Seven Mile Bridge — the road that went to sea*

encounter. The grand finale is a trip on their 'bottomless boat', where visitors and dolphins go for a short cruise. To get even closer take a Dolphin Encounter session (which should be pre-booked).

The State Park Tour Boat leaves from MM 79, taking in two interesting keys which Henry Flagler's epic railroad missed. Early morning cruises are to **Indian Key**. Many of the tropical plants thriving on the island were established by physician and botanist Dr Henry Perrin, who died during an Indian attack which reversed the island's fortunes. Florida Park Rangers now give tours of this historic island, and also **Lignumvitae Key**, which boasts an almost pristine hammock. The Key was named after the Lignum Vitae, the 'wood of life', a hardwood highly prized by the early Spanish and later settlers. The tour also encompasses the Matheson House, constructed of coral rock, plus its cistern and a windmill which generated electricity. Period furnishing and utensils depict early island life. Since both islands are accessible only by boat, they offer tranquil settings to explore the keys. Divers can also visit San Pedro Underwater State park, part of the Spanish treasure fleet disaster. The 18ft of water allows viewing by more adventurous snorkelers, and the site has been enhanced by replica cannons and other artifacts.

Return to Highway 1 and **Long Key State Park**. Popular park pastimes include walking the Golden Orb Nature Trail, named after the harmless spider which decorates the shrubbery along the pathway. Other activities include camping (tenters may ask for the walk-in sites, which are further from the road), canoeing a water trail, fishing (licence required), and of course picnicking.

## Marathon Environs

After a few more islands is Grassy Key and the **Dolphin Research Center**, marked as the Flipper Sea School on older maps. The site's dolphin habitat was originally created by Milton Santini, who lacked funds for an expensive aquarium and thus chose the ocean as a more natural environment. His trained dolphins were used for the Flipper movies, which sparked the popular television series. Although the low barrier is an easy dolphin jump away from Florida Bay and freedom, these sociable marine mammals have grown up with human contact and return to their five-star dolphin hotel.

Visitors are taken on an interesting, educational tour, while the dolphins titter amongst themselves and scrutinize the audience or come forward to help demonstrate some of their unique abilities. The fee helps the non-profit research center in many ways: public awareness and education, hospitalization, rehabilitation and/or a retirement home for dolphins, whether rescued in the wild or suffering trauma related to long periods in an aquarium. Keen 'Dolfriends' may have an encounter with one of the more gregarious inhabitants, or attend the week-long Dolphinlab, but the waiting list is long.

The **Museum of Natural History of the Florida Keys** is situated at MM 50.5. The museum is surrounded by Crane Point Hammock, recently rescued by the Florida Keys Land and Sea Trust from becoming yet another shopping mall. Rather than display heaps of dusty artifacts the museum has gone for fewer high quality exhibits which punctuate the rather flamboyant history of the Keys. A children's museum is the latest addition, while the hammock itself preserves tropical hardwoods, evidence of the pre-Columbian Calusa Indians, and an early settlement of Bahamians.

**Marathon** itself is a growing community, with airport connections to Miami and Fort Lauderdale, and yet more resorts, marinas, and Tiki bars. They run a trio of fishing tournaments in November, while the Keys Art League and the Marathon Art Guild are busiest exhibiting during the winter months. Beyond Marathon is the longest stretch of water on US Highway 1.

**Seven Mile Bridge** is billed as a major attraction, but the star has to be the peacock-coloured sea which surrounds it. The old bridge, once part of Flagler's railway, only goes as far as Pigeon Key. This tiny sub-tropical isle still boasts the old style conch homes, but do not detour for them. They, and the old bridge, are better appreciated from the main highway. Long time residents in the Keys, the self-styled conchs (pronounced konks), love to reminisce about driving down the narrow old seven mile bridge and meeting an oncoming Greyhound Bus. 'More atheists got a sudden dose of religion on that bridge than in any ol' church!' The new bridge is not nearly so adventurous, and drivers can sneak a careful glance over the railing.

**Bahia Honda State Recreation Area** has the best beach on the Keys. Activities include diving and snorkeling, both popular pastimes on the boat trip to the nearby Looe Key National Marine Sanctuary. You can also rent wind surfers, or buy T-Shirts, bait, and lunch. Day-use visitors should arrive early during winter and spring, while campers should book as far ahead as possible (maximum 2 months). The six cabin units are also popular, especially on weekends and holidays.Rangers conduct guided walks during the peak season (call for times). Many 'rare' birds are commonly spotted on the Keys, including Audubon's beloved white-crowned pigeon.

**Big Pine Key** is best known for the endangered Key Deer which inhabit the surrounding islands. Although related to the Virginia white-tailed deer, these tiny creatures reach a shoulder height of 24 to 28in, and are often mistaken for dogs. Big Pine Key is the least developed of the larger Keys, but loss of habitat and automobile accidents are major contributors to the declining Key Deer, and only some 250 remain. Visitors are asked to drive cautiously: politely by the signs, and more emphatically by the traffic officers. Rather surprisingly, the Key Deer Sanctuary — which should protect the deer — is a public use area riddled with roads. Another refuge which surrounds many Keys is the Great White Heron National Wildlife Refuge. Access without a boat is difficult, but Reflections Nature Tours make things easy by providing an experienced guide, equipment, and a light lunch. Those without time to tour can still search for the Great White Heron while travelling through the Keys — these birds look like unusually large white egrets, but have yellow legs *and* beaks.

The **Looe Key Reef Resort** at MM 27.5 is a diver's paradise, although non-divers are also welcome to stay at the hotel and swim in the pool. They operate a five-star PADI training facility, which is combined with easy access to the Looe Key National Marine Sanctuary. Beginners will find the reef resort an ideal place and visiting divers are given briefings on reef ecology, protecting the coral, and preserving the treasures (yes, there is a sunken ship) for future dives.

Take time to appreciate the less developed lower islands, because Key West is fast approaching. Keep an eagle-eye out for birds of prey such as the osprey, whose deep nests sit upon boxes atop tall poles. The white headed and breasted ospreys are often mistaken for bald eagles, which also may be seen along Highway 1.

## Crazy Key West

Cosmopolitan Key West is utterly unlike the other Keys. Originally named *Cayo Hueso* or 'Bone Island', for the human remains left by an Indian battle (or cannibals), the name was Anglicized to West. At various times the island was a haven for pirates, Bahamians, Cuban refugees, Greek spongers, and wreckers. The latter risked their lives in the lucrative business of salvaging ships sunk by hurricanes and treacherous reefs, all too common off southern Florida. During the heyday of wrecking, Key West had the highest income per person of any city in Florida and allegedly of the United States. Since those days Key West has been embraced by many others, including artists and archaeologists, dropouts and developers. All have left their mark on Key West, especially the latter, which includes the American Navy. New Key West was born of various land fills and drainage schemes, almost quadrupling the area of habitable land.

**Old Key West** was incorporated long before the railroad or highway reached the islands. Perhaps that is why Key West has so many

*Canoeists tour the Great White Heron Refuge at Big Pine Key*

*Tropical shopping is best at Key West*

interesting side streets. Roosevelt Boulevard circles New Key West, while downtown is a crisscross of narrow streets and alleys overhung by tropical trees. Key West makes a refreshing change from the strip development along Highway 1. Since parking is at a premium in the Old Town, some prefer to park at the Key West Visitor Center or across from the Old Town Trolley headquarters on Northern Roosevelt Boulevard (US 1) and take a tour in. The sunset performances and Key West nightlife are prime attractions, and should not be missed, so at least one night in Key West is a must. Parking can be a nuisance downtown, but several bike rental companies line Duval Street, and Old Key West is not too large to be walked.

**Mallory Square** is the heart of Old Key West. Both the Conch Tour Train and the Old Town Trolley leave from there, and they provide an excellent introuction to Key West, plus discount vouchers for many attractions. The open-sided Conch Tour Train provides an atmospheric $1^1/_2$-hour tour of Key West, new and old. The Old Town Trolley runs every half hour. Unlike the Conch Tour Train it stops at specified points of interest and provides on/off privileges.

Also in Mallory Square is Hospitality House, run by the Old Island Restoration Foundation. Their free brochure describing a walking tour known as the 'Pelican Path' has a detailed map of Old Key West. One need not follow the entire tour, indeed many of the houses described are not open to the public, but several sites, including the Hemingway and Audubon houses, should be visited if time permits.

Near the square is the Key West Chamber of Commerce with information on local sites, current events and accommodation. Nearby is **Mallory Market**, with its shell warehouse, sponge market, and T-shirt stores. Their **Key West Aquarium** has colourful fish in large tanks, a petting area and exhibits of live coral. Children also love spotting the sharks, rays and turtles.

After a hundred miles of just the one major highway, the streets of Key West can be disorienting. Front Street is easy, since it runs in *front* of Mallory Square. Almost perpendicular to Front Street is **Duval Street**, noted both for good shopping and nightlife. It has been claimed as the longest street in the world because it runs from the Atlantic Ocean to the Gulf of Mexico! Mallory Square is at the gulf end of Duval Street, while the Atlantic beaches are east from the other end. Simonton Street, one block north of Duval, is another popular 'shopping experience'. Bright island styles are the order of the day at Key West Hand Print Fabrics and Fashions.

A short walk from Mallory Square can take in numerous points of interest, including the Fireball Glassbottom Boat, which takes regular trips from the gulf end of Duval Street. **Mel Fisher's Maritime**

**Heritage Museum** is west from Mallory Square on Green Street. Mel Fisher belongs to a new breed of wreckers, who search for sunken treasure using ancient historic records and the latest high-tech equipment. Mel became exceedingly wealthy after his discovery of the *Atocha*, once part of the Spanish plate fleets. Although bearing Mel Fisher's name the Maritime Heritage Museum is run by a non-profit organization dedicated to preserving artifacts from the *Atocha* and other wrecks. They present both the history and the finds, including some beautiful examples of the gold and jewelry. Behind the museum gift shop is another, far more expensive one, which *is* owned by Mel Fisher, where actual artifacts from the wrecks are sold.

On Whitehead Street, which runs parallel and to the south of Duval, is the **Audubon House and Gardens**. The house once belonged to a harbour pilot and wrecker who befriended John James Audubon. The latter was compiling his *Birds of America*, and while travelling the Keys discovered eighteen new species, including the great white heron. Another, the white-crowned pigeon, was painted in the garden, although it is likely that Audubon never slept at the house. Fortunately the house and gardens were saved from destruction and gradually restored. The Florida Audubon Society operate the museum, which displays rare Audubon engravings and period furnishings. Inclusive in the admission fee is an excellent self-guided tour which highlights the many tropical plants within the garden, and their uses.

The **Wrecker's Museum**, sometime entitled the Oldest House, also relives the heyday of wrecking. The furnishings are not as elaborate as the Audubon House, and reflect the lifestyle of the earlier wreckers. In those days the wooden houses had separate kitchens, a protection against heat and the dangers of fire, and the museum kitchen is one of the few survivors. Part of the Old City Hall on Greene Street has been given over to the **Historic Key West Shipwreck Museum**. Given the treacherous reefs and dangers from hurricanes and squalls, the emphasis on wrecking is hardly surprising, but the museum highlights the dangers and rewards of salvage itself, rather than the lifestyle of the wrecker. Many of the artifacts are from the American merchant ship *Isaac Allerton*.

While many artists and writers have embraced Key West, Ernest Hemingway still haunts the island. *To Have and Have Not* is based upon his years at Key West, seemingly all spent at Sloppy Joe's Bar according to local legend. He also wrote *A Farewell to Arms, Green Hills of Africa, For Whom the Bell Tolls*, and other notable novels at his home in Key West. After his death the new owners of the **Ernest Hemingway Home** discovered considerable interest in the author, so the house and grounds were dedicated to his memory. Tours of the home, gardens, and Hemingway's private writing loft are given by knowledgeable guides. Tales of Key West's only cellar, the excavated coral rock being used to construct the house, and the Key's first swimming pool, where his second wife spent Hemingway's 'last penny', make fascinating listening. But the Hemingway legend is not without some basis, and descendents of Ernest's six-toed cats still live within the gardens.

The Hemingway home is a good walk down Whitehead Street, or a short hop from the Trolley Bus stop. Nearby is the **Key West Lighthouse Museum**, with excellent views atop the 86ft climb. The keeper's house is now a museum of the maritime history of Key West. Another Trolley stop takes in **East Martello Tower Museum & Gallery**. Constructed as a part of the Coastal Defence Network, the tower was outdated before it was completed. It now houses exhibits giving a comprehensive history, heritage, and the life of Old Key West, including Flagler's railway and the works of local artisans. While no one of royal lineage has ever been held captive in the tower, the structure is usefully protecting the world from the imaginative creations of Stanley Papio. Originally a welder, Stanley used scrap metal to good effect, and his garden became an outdoor 'junk art' museum. His neighbours had him arrested on six occasions, but he continued to enhance his collection of metal men and women, who now reside in the East Martello Tower Museum and gardens.

**Fort Zachary Taylor** is one of the most elusive sites within Key West. Accessible only from Southard Street through the US Naval Air Station, the walls of the much modified fort contain the largest collection of artifacts from the American Civil War. The fort was continuously altered as weapon technology progressed, and the ramparts were strengthened by concrete poured over antiquated Civil War canons. Today the different sections illustrate the changing arts of fortifications, and many uncovered artifacts are on exhibit. The area is also popular for picnicking and getting away from the bustle of Key West proper.

**Fort Jefferson National Monument** is out on the Dry Tortugas, a short hop by seaplane or a pleasant ride by charter boat. The expense keeps many away, so visitors may explore the fort, snorkel the sparkling waters, and birdwatch from an area little disturbed by humans. Take binoculars, sun protection (clothing and cream), cool drinks or water, and a picnic lunch.

A popular place to visit is the **Key West City Cemetery**. The trolley tour passes but does not stop here, but with comfortable shoes and plenty of time one can walk down Duval Street and turn left on

Angela Street. Pause at the entrance to admire the bottle wall, constructed of carefully consumed bottles of many different colours. Wandering around the cemetery is such fun that guided tours are provided on weekends at 10am and 4pm. Among the memorials is one to the Cuban martyrs of the Bay of Pigs invasion, and another to those who died when the USS *Maine* was sunk in Havana, sparking off the Spanish-American War. Those visiting the site during the week should not miss one peculiar message found on a family crypt near the B'NAI ZION entrance. The humorous inscription on B. P. Roberts' tombstone is pure Key West, as she gets the last laugh — 'I told you I was sick.'

✳ Towards the end of day everyone returns to **Mallory Pier**, for the world famous Sunset Celebration. Teams of streetwise performers stake out their territory about an hour before sunset, and their spectacle is like walking through Barnum's circus. The Cat Man puts his domesticated friends through the same paces as the big cats, including the hoop of fire. A bagpiper begins a lament, while an appreciative audience gathers around Bimbo, the-larger-than-life clown with an artistic knack with balloons. Jugglers rub elbows with sword swallowers, while the chants of the Cookie Lady weave spells. If the sunset is spectacular enough everyone applauds, and the crowd gradually dissipates.

*Spanish Gold at the Maritime Heritage Museum*

By nightfall everyone has regrouped at their favourite bar or nightspot. **Sloppy Joe's Bar** is on the corner of Duval and Greene. This is not the legendary Sloppy Joe's where Ernest Hemingway drank, although Hemingway did imbibe here, too. Sloppy Joe Russel moved his business when Hemingway's fame caused the rent to increase. It was the nearby **Captain Tony's** which Hemingway actually frequented, when *it* was called Sloppy Joe's Bar. But names are unimportant in Key West, and the ghosts of yesteryear will not buy a round of drinks today. Each nightspot collects a different crowd: some like a Cuban beat, others jazz, '50s, '60s, or good old-fashioned country music.

## *Additional Information*

### *Visitor Information*

Florida Keys & Key West Visitors
  Bureau
PO Box 1147
Key West FL 33041-1147
☎ 305-296-3811 or 800-FLA-KEYS

### *Local Events*

*1 Jan-30 Apr*
Key West's Old Island Days
Key West

*Mid Jan*
Florida Keys Renaissance Faire
Marathon

Upper Keys Seafood Festival
Key Largo

*Mid March*
Rail Barrel Arts Festival
Islamorada

*Mid July*
Hemingway Days Festival
Key West

*Mid to end Oct*
Fantasy Fest
Key West

*Early to mid Nov*
Island Jubilee
Key Largo

### *Places of Interest*

**Big Pine Key**
*Bahia Honda State Recreation Area*
Route 1, Box 782
FL 33043
☎ 305-872-2353
Open: 8am-sunset
Beach, swim, picnic, nature trail, camp, ♿

**Grassy Key**
*Dolphin Research Center*
PO Box Dolphin (US Hwy 1)
Marathon Shores FL 33052
☎ 305-289-1121 or 0002
Open: Wed-Sun. Gifts, ♿

**Islamorada**
*Theater of the Sea*
Mile Marker 84.5, US Highway 1
FL 33036
☎ 305-664-2431
Open: 9.0am-4pm. Gifts, tour, ♿

**Key Largo**
*John Pennekamp Coral Reef State Park*
Post Office Box 487
(Mile Marker 102.5)
FL 33037
☎ 305-451-1202
Open: 8am-sunset
Swim, snorkel, picnic/camp/fish, scuba lessons, rental

## Key West

*Audubon House*
205 Whitehead St
FL 33040
☎ 305-294-2116
Open: 9.30am-5pm
Tour, Audubon art, garden

*East Martello Gallery and Museum*
3501 S Roosevelt Blvd
FL 33040
☎ 304-296-3913
Open: 9.30am-5pm except Xmas
Civil war fort, art gallery, gifts

*Fort Zachary Taylor Historic Site*
PO Box 289
(west end of Southard St)
FL 33041
☎ 305-292-6713
Open: 8am-sunset. Guided tours
daily at 2pm
Historic fort, tours, picnic

*Hemingway Home and Museum*
907 Whitehead St
FL 33040
☎ 305-294-1575
Open: 9am-5pm
Guided tours, six-toed cats

*Key West Lighthouse Museum*
938 Whitehead St
FL 33040
☎ 305-294-0012
Open: 9.0am-5.30pm
Gifts

*Mallory Market*
Mallory Square
FL 33040
☎ 305-294-5168
Open: 9am-late daily
Admission fee for aquarium only
Shopping, aquarium, snacks

*Mel Fisher Maritime Heritage
   Society's Treasure Museum*
200 Greene St
FL 33040
☎ 305-294-9936
Open: 10am-5.15pm
Gifts, ♿

*Wrecker's Museum*
(Oldest house in Key West)
322 Duval St
FL 33040
☎ 305-294-9502
Open: 10am-4pm
Guided tours

## Long Key

*Long Key State Recreation Area*
PO Box 776 (US Highway 1)
FL 33001
☎ 305-664-4815
Open: 8am-sunset
Camp, nature walk, limited
swimmming, ♿

## Marathon

*Crane Point Hammock*
Mile Marker 50, PO Box 536
FL 33050
☎ 305-743-9100
Open: 9am-5pm Wed-Mon, 9am-
8pm Fri
Natural history & children's
museum, nature walk, ♿

## *Tours and Transportation*

## Key West

*Conch Tour Train*
601 Duval St, Suite 8
(Trains from Mallory Square)
FL 33040
☎ 305-294-5161
$1\frac{1}{2}$ hour tour, 9am-4pm

*Key West Seaplane Service*
5603 Jr College Road
FL 33040
☎ 305-294-6978
Hours vary
Air tours to Fort Jefferson

*Old Town Trolley Tours*
PO Box 1237
(Board at 1910 North Roosevelt or
Mallory Sq)
FL 33041
☎ 305-296-6688
$1\frac{1}{2}$ hour tour 8.55am-4.30pm.
On/off privileges.

# 3

# *THE EVERGLADES*

*Pa-Hay-Okee*, or Grassy Waters, was the descriptive Indian name for the Everglades. Although comprised of many interdependent ecosystems, the main feature of the Everglades is the 50 mile (80km) wide 'River of Grass'. It takes two days for the water to flow through a mile of grassy savannah, dropping, on average, just one inch.

The rainwater which once fed the Everglades came from as far away as Orlando, carried into Lake Okeechobee by the Kissimmee River, but today the water must also quench other needs. Almost two thousand miles of canals and levees have drained and irrigated the land surrounding Okeechobee, the fourth largest lake wholly in the United States. To the north of the huge lake are thousands of tons of prime beef cattle, while the rich muck soil along the lake's southern rim produces one third of America's sugar crop. Add a burgeoning population along both the gulf and Atlantic coastlines, and water must be used and re-used to meet the demand.

The Everglades of today is said to be facing its greatest danger ever. After a campaign which included rousing speeches by centenarian Marjory Stoneman Douglas, whose *The Everglades — River of Grass* contributed significantly to the formation of the Everglades National Park, President George Bush signed a Bill in late 1989 which ecologists hope will save *Pa-Hay-Okee*. The East Everglades will eventually be added, while the US Army Corps of Engineers promise to 'put right' the system of water management levees and canals. Perhaps by the twenty-first century there will be a better dispersed, more natural flow into the Everglades.

## The Everglades Main Park Entrance

The **Everglades National Park** encompasses 1.4 million acres, and  provides a representative cross-section of the entire Everglades

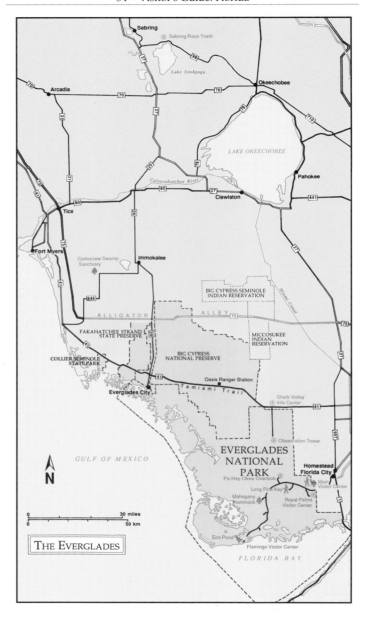

THE EVERGLADES

ecosystem. Most visitors enter the park at the **Main Entrance** near Homestead, some 50 miles (80km) southwest of Miami. From the entrance the road runs 38 miles (61km) to Flamingo, with numerous points of interest. Unfortunately the first-time visitor may be underwhelmed by the broad savannah punctuated with clumps of trees. Certainly the Everglades exhibits an almost total apathy to those who drive directly to Flamingo without once leaving their cars.

To enjoy a more fruitful Everglades experience, visitors should really begin to appreciate their surroundings *before* reaching the entrance. From the end of the Florida Turnpike Extension at Homestead, Highway 9336 meanders past crops of avocado, corn, strawberries, and miles of tomatoes, ripening in the Florida sun. The flat dusty soil was once part of the Everglades, but the area now produces fresh vegetables by the truckload for Greater Miami and beyond. Prices at the roadside vary from impossibly cheap to twice the supermarket average, and the energetic may pick their own.

The surroundings change so gradually that some drivers miss the main visitor center, which is located before the entrance kiosk. The

*These Everglades air plants are related to the pineapple*

*The anhinga, or snake bird, must dry after feeding*

introductory movie is shown regularly at the visitor center. Interpretive exhibits help the visitor to appreciate the more subtle beauty which is the Everglades. It is worth calling ahead for information on special activities, such as guided nature walks, canoe trips, and swamp walks. During the cooler months the rangers have several programs daily at Royal Palm, Flamingo, Shark Valley, and Everglades City. To help out-of-state visitors reservations may not be made more than two days ahead. Naturalists are on hand to answer questions, and their advice on nature's spectacle, which varies with season and rainfall, is invaluable. The visitor centre is the last place before Flamingo to buy mosquito repellant.

The entrance ticket, valid for seven days, may also be used at the entrance at Shark Valley. Beyond the kiosk is the turnoff to the **Royal Palms Visitor Center**, a marvellous introduction to the Everglades, with two nature walks highlighting the park's incredible diversity. The Anhinga Trail is named after the unusual waterbird which frequents the area. Sometimes called the water turkey or snake bird, the anhinga has a long, serpentine neck and sharply pointed beak to spear its prey. The transfixed fish is brought to the surface, and with a practiced toss the snake bird catches and swallows the victim headfirst. The anhinga resembles the cormorant, another fishing bird on the trail, but the cormorant has a broader neck and a hooked beak. Herons and egrets also frequent the grassy banks and water's edge, as do the alligators, who sun themselves on the bank or float almost invisibly in the water. The name alligator comes from the Spanish *El Legarto*, which simply means the lizard.

Nearby is the Gumbo Limbo Trail, a short walk through a hammock or high spot. Despite being adjacent to the water-filled, grass covered Taylor Slough, which the Anhinga Trail boardwalk goes over, the few extra feet in height utterly changes the character of the trail. Sunlight scarcely reaches the forest floor, as hardwood trees form an overhead canopy festooned with vines and creepers — a tropical rain forest without the celestial waterfall. The Gumbo Limbo trees have a reddish, peeling bark, which has occasioned their other name, the Tourist Tree, after the sunburnt Florida visitors.

Further along the main park road is another turnoff, to **Long Pine Key**. In addition to picnic facilities, there is a large, primitive camping area (no electricity), and a network of longer walks. Trails through another Everglades ecosystem, the pineland forests, range from a 3 mile (4.8km) loop to the 14 mile (22.5km) Long Pine Key Nature Trail. Many other plants grow under the thinner canopy of the slash pine, which are immune to the periodic fires which control the undergrowth. The area supports white-tailed deer, a vital food source for the almost extinct Florida panther. Those with little time may miss the trip to Long Pine Key and take the half-mile Pineland Trail, with a briefer introduction to pineland ecology.

Beyond the turnoff to Pine Glades Lake, terminus to the Long Pine Key Nature Trail, the land changes once more. The pinelands give way to grassy areas punctuated by forests of stunted bald cypress. Rock Reef Pass is situated on a limestone ridge just 3ft above sea level. Higher still is the man-made structure called **Pa-Hay-Okee Overlook**, where the romantic see a wondrous vista of unending savannah. Others find the great expanse of the Shark River Slough an incredible bore where, no matter how long one looks, nothing seems to happen. Unlike other short trails within the Everglades, the overlook is not accessible to wheelchairs, due to a stairway.

There are no restrictions against leaving the road and wandering off into the Everglades by foot or canoe, and the overnight camping permit is free. During the wet season the alligator holes are difficult to spot, as are the creatures which made them, with other pitfalls too numerous to mention. On the other hand, a short foray across 'dry' prairie can be very instructive, but protect feet and ankles from sharp limestone and hidden holes. Ficus and Sweet Bay Ponds are marked on the free Everglades National Park Map, but the paths are not.  Walking tracks to the ponds can be spotted by the 'No vehicles beyond this point' warning signs. Both paths are short walks over Marl Prairie, where the thin, clay-like soil is pierced occasionally by the rough limestone base.

The best example of a hardwood community may be seen at **Mahogany Hammock**, which has the largest extant mahogany tree in the United States. Orchids can be difficult to recognize unless in bloom, while the strangler fig is one of the more interesting inhabitants of the hammock. The seeds grow from wherever birds, which eat the fruit, deposit them, such as on a tree limb. The 'strangler' lives as an air plant until its aerial roots reach the ground. A proper root system is then formed, and the fig gradually kills the host tree by blotting out its sunlight. Taking samples from trees, whether peeling bark or otherwise, is both prohibited and unwise, unless one can correctly identify the poisonwood tree!

Mahogany Hammock is roughly halfway to Flamingo. Beyond is another section with longer walks, and also the first canoe trails. Otherwise press on to Flamingo, pausing at Mrazek Pond to check for the bird life which often congregates there. At Flamingo canoes  (and racks to carry them on your vehicle) may be rented, but advance bookings are recommended in the busy winter season. Also check with park rangers before embarking on any particular canoe trail that the water levels are high enough. At the Pearl Bay Chickee,there is camping overnight in the wild where physically handicapped canoeists have access and priority.

First amongst the canoe trails is Nine Mile Pond, which is actually just over 5 miles (8km) round trip. This is a very scenic trail over an area where outboard motors are prohibited, with plenty of wildlife but difficult to navigate. The Hells Bay Canoe Trail was so called because it was 'Hell to get in, and Hell to get out.' The shelter at Pearl Bay is 3.5 miles (5.6km) each way, while Hells Bay is a 10 mile (16km) round trip. Motors are prohibited over much of the trail, primarily because they would be useless through the mangrove-lined sections. The Westlake Canoe Trail is 7.7 miles (12.5km) each way to the primitive campsite at Alligator Creek, and one paddles through good crocodile and alligator habitat. Other trips which do not require transporting canoes by cartop are available from Flamingo.

The first walk beyond Mahogany Hammock is the short but informative West Lake Nature Trail, a boardwalk under a mangrove canopy lining the shallow lakes. Florida's commercial and recreational fishing industries rely heavily on mangrove-lined estuaries for breeding, and the tree is one of the most protected in Florida.

The Snake Bight Trail sounds dangerous until one realizes that bight means bay within a bay; the tour tram from Flamingo follows the same 3.2 mile (5km) trail. Birdwatching can be good from the boardwalk's terminus, which overlooks the bay, depending upon tide and season. The Rowdy Bend Trail follows an old roadway through buttonwood forest and the more open coastal prairie, created where hurricanes flattened sections of woodland. The trail is 2.6 miles (4.6km) each way, or one may pick up the Snake Bight Trail and then return by road for a round trip. The Christian Point Trail, 3.5 miles (5.6km) round trip, leads through more buttonwood to a different point along the Snake Bight coast. This is the last trail before the Flamingo Visitor Center.

**Mrazek Pond** is located after the Snake Bight Trailhead, and is probably the best known birdwatching site in the Everglades National Park, due to its proximity to the roadside. Winter is the main spotting season, as birds escaping the frozen north swell the local bird population. At these times the pond swarms with birdwatchers and professional photographers, who make as interesting viewing as the birds themselves.

A short walk beyond the Flamingo Visitors Center is **Eco Pond**. Although only a few dozen yards from the roadside, the birds are protected from car-bound visitors — it is considered it to be *the* place to spot birds. Early morning guided walks are popular there, while

*In the Everglades photographers are not an endangered species*

Do not feed or molest wildlife

*Alligators are best observed from the safety of boardwalk trails*

the keenest watchers arrive at dawn. Only parts of the pond are visible from any one point, and you may be rewarded with rare woodland birds or raptors as well as waterfowl.

Flamingos are one species visitors are unlikely to see at **Flamingo Visitor Center**. Early residents needed a place name to receive mail, and someone thought Flamingo had an exotic ring. But the old settlement is long gone, and even the park road is mostly a new addition. Facilities include the visitor center itself, with rangers to answer questions, and wildlife exhibits with carved wooden replicas of the local fauna. The park service also manages the large campground which, like Long Pine Key, has no electricity or water plumbed to the RV sites. Rangers hold regular evening talks at the amphitheatre near the tent area, and everyone is invited, whether camping or not. The tent area is a short walk from the parking lot, making set-up much easier. Also 'Clarence', an alligator who alternates between Eco Pond and Florida Bay, may stroll through the area at night, so do follow recommendations against feeding the alligators or keeping food in tents.

**Flamingo Lodge** provides clean, comfortable rooms at prices regulated by the National Park Service. There are sufficient activities at Flamingo to justify spending a night or two there, and even day visitors or campers are allowed to make use of resort facilities, including the screened swimming pool. Self-catering cabins are also available, with fully equipped kitchens and beds for four or six people. Several are accessible for the handicapped, and these are automatically booked when asking for a room with wheelchair access, so they get a cabin for the price of a room. A year-round snack bar supplements the restaurant, which has an excellent menu but is open only during winter and early spring, when Flamingo Lodge even caters for conventions and weddings. Outside these months the mosquitos become very fierce, and Homestead is a better base.

The mosquito-resistant Tram Tour (winter only) takes visitors from the resort down the Snake Bight Trail, highlighting the land-based flora and fauna. There are organized boat tours of Florida Bay or the backcountry canals and lakes. The former is better for bird spotting, especially during the sunset trip when flocks pass overhead en route to their rookeries. The latter goes up the Flamingo Canal, which is separated from Florida Bay by a plug to help slow the salt water intrusion into the Everglades. The meandering, mangrove-lined Whitewater Bay is over 10 miles (16km) long, and connects with the Snake River, part of the Wilderness Waterway.

 For independent adventurers, the marina hires canoes and small boats with outboard motors. The latter are only allowed into the backcountry, weather permitting. Since Buttonwood Canal is 3 miles (4.8km) long, and some sections are no-wake zones to protect the endangered manatee, allow several hours or more to make the rental worthwhile. Canoeists in the backcountry must contend with the privately owned, overpowered bass boats which roar down Buttonwood Canal. There is a detour part way down the canal onto the Bear Lake Canoe Trail which the fishing boats cannot follow, since it requires a short portage. For a short trip, Florida Bay may offer better canoeing. At low tide at the Flamingo Marina numerous birds can be seen feeding in the shallow water; with a canoe one may get much closer. Among the brown pelicans are larger American white pelicans, egrets, heron and roseate spoonbills, while ibis also frequent the area, especially in winter and early spring. Landing on the mangrove islands is not permitted, since they are some of the last habitat available for large bird rookeries. Warning signs keep canoeists well away from an island where bald eagles are nesting. Those interested in travelling the Wilderness Waterway, 90 miles (145km) of backwater paddling, should allow a week. Unless they have all requisites for canoeing and camping in the wild for a week, plus a friend to pick them up at the other end, they should contact North American Canoe Tours in Everglades City.

Bicycles are also popular, and may be hired. The Coastal Prairie trail is 7 miles (11km) each way, and bikes are probably advisable unless one is camping there (permit required, and watch out for no-see-ums, bugs that bite unseen). The trail leaves from behind the campground and, before the canals were dug, continued on to Cape Sable. Near Flamingo Lodge is a well stocked gift shop, which also sells tickets for the Trolley Tour which embarks there. Water based activities such as boat tours and rentals are at the marina, which is just before the lodge and cannot be missed. Ticket queues become longest just before a tour departs, so arrive early, even if a tour is reserved. The marina general store sells almost anything a camper, boater, cabin resident, or casual visitor could possibly need.

## Tamiami Trail — Another Everglades

Despite the name, there is little to see along Alligator Alley, the highway which connects East Florida with West. The same is true for the parallel extension of Interstate 75; both routes are about crossing the Everglades quickly. For interesting sights, plus access to other sections of the Everglades National Park, take the Tamiami Trail. Also called Highway 41, the name is a contraction of Tampa to Miami, and we are concerned with the Miami to Naples section.

The Tamiami Trail leaves Miami from Little Havana, the Cuban enclave. Eventually the roadside becomes rural, and waterfowl may be seen along the Tamiami Canal. Alligators also frequent the canal, dug to drain the Everglades and to provide fill for constructing the trail. Numerous billboards along this stretch advertise airboat tours, which are generally better on the northern side (right while driving away from Miami), because of the higher water levels. Although many people associate airboats with the Everglades, they are not allowed within the park boundaries, but then again, the park covers less than a third of the original *Pa-Hay-Okee*.

The heart of the Everglades is accessible via **Shark Valley**, the northern entrance to the National Park. The Shark Valley Slough (shallow waterway) eventually reaches Florida Bay via the Shark River. The main attraction is the ranger-guided tram tour, a 15 mile (24km) informative excursion through the river of grass from the comfort of a paved roadway. During the dryer months of winter the water level normally drops below the surrounding land, and any remaining water holes are excellent places to spot birds, otter, and alligators. During the late spring to autumn the slough is fed by dramatic thunderstorms, and flows slowly once more. The many species of fish, and the animals which prey upon them, fan out to the horizon and beyond, making them more difficult to spot. The tour pauses at the tall observatory tower, which is accessible by wheelchair up a long ramp. There are nature trails near the park entrance, and the loop road may also be travelled on foot, although a bicycle, which the park rents, will be preferable for the complete trip.

The Everglades are home to a growing number of Miccosukee Indians, many working at the **Miccosukee Indian Village**. The restaurant here and the Miccosukee Information Center are across the road from the Shark Valley Entrance. From the air-conditioned restaurant one may spot alligators, great blue herons, and snowy egrets, while trying tourist versions of Indian food. The airboat tours here are better than many, as the stepped seats give rear passengers a good view. The leisurely tram tour at Shark Valley contrasts sharply with the roar and rush of the airboat. At full tilt the prolific wildlife rockets past, but the Indian guides do pause occasionally and an Indian hammock is visited. The village itself has regular guided tours to show the Miccosukee way of life. Trinkets on sale include artifacts that tourists expect *all* Indians to sell, but items like the dolls and patchwork are local Miccosukee. The quality of dolls and clothing in general may be judged by the inclusion of what the Miccosukee (and Seminoles) do best — colourful, intricate patchwork. Used patchwork skirts and jackets are collectors' items, even among the Indians. Miccosukee grandmothers still make (or buy)

*Miccosukee airboat captain wearing a typical patchwork jacket*

*The swamp-loving cypress trees have air-breathing 'knees'*

beautifully crafted clothing for favourite grandchildren. Skirts and jackets on sale should be examined for the intricacy of the patchwork and quality of stitching. Do not expect to buy designs seen in history museums, as patchwork styles are constantly changing.

Beyond Miccosukee Village is the 1.4 million acre **Big Cypress National Preserve**, much of which adjoins the Everglades National Park. The Oasis Ranger Station is the main interpretive center, with films, exhibits, and volunteers who answer questions. That, and driving through it, is the extent to which most passers-by enjoy the Big Cypress Preserve. A section of the Florida Trail leaves from behind the Oasis Visitor Center, but one has to be well prepared to travel very far on it. The trail runs 29 miles (47km) to Alligator Alley, with no pick-up service. Those in rental cars should be aware they are *not* covered by insurance while travelling down dirt side roads. Bone shattering, wheel-damaging, off-road driving is prohibited to everything except specially equipped vehicles.

# Everglades via the Gulf Coast

Barron G. Collier was the developer who built the Tamiami Trail, and he had considerable help from the Seminole (and Miccosukee) Indians, who could withstand the hardships of building a road through a trackless swamp. It is fitting that **Collier Seminole State Park** combines their names. The park straddles portions of the Big Cypress Swamp and the coastal mangrove wilderness. The park offers an excellent boardwalk nature trail which includes a hardwood hammock and mangrove environments. Stately royal palms grow there naturally and, untypical of the stereotype developer, Barron Collier wished to preserve their beauty. There is a monument to Collier, a replica Seminole War blockhouse which doubles as an interpretive center, and a massive dredge which was used to build the Tamiami Trail. During the winter months (fewer troublesome insects) the adventurous can walk the northern section of the park on a 6.5 mile (11km) hiking trail. The loop walk goes through some pristine habitat, where even the black bear may be found. The mangrove wilderness may be explored by rental canoe. Paddle trips need not be long, although there is a 13.5 mile (22km) canoe trail with backcountry camping for those have the requisite equipment. Only a limited number of visitors are allowed to travel the waterways per day, which heightens the feeling of wilderness.

South of the Tamiami Trail on Highway 29 is **Everglades City**. Every year brings a new airboat or swamp buggy tour, and the Chamber of Commerce Visitor Center, located on the junction of Highways 29 and 41, provides coffee (donations accepted) while they help visitors chose a tour. Eden of the Everglades provide narrated boat tours of the mangrove waterways, and their operation has a rustic, pioneering atmosphere. Everglades National Park Boat Tours provide additional excursions by boat, while Wootens, out on the Tamiami, offer airboat and swamp buggy trips into the Everglades, but not the actual park. For a true wilderness experience, try the North American Canoe Tours Everglades Outpost. They rent canoes by the hour, day, and also offer a complete delivery and, where required, pick-up service. The Everglades Wilderness Waterway is only one of many trips they organize, with or without accompanying guides, alone or in groups.

## Everglades Excursions from the Gulf Coast

After Everglades City, the Tamiami Trail heads north up the Gulf Coast to Tampa. Everglades City, Collier Seminole State Park, and Shark Valley are popular day trips from the resorts which line the coast from Tampa/St Petersburg through Fort Myers to sunny Naples. Another option for those along the Gulf of Mexico, often missed by drivers rushing to the Everglades, is **Corkscrew Swamp Sanctuary**. The National Audubon Society have preserved the largest extant stand of virgin bald cypress in the world. A self-guided boardwalk tour, accessible by wheelchair, winds through swamp, hammock, and 'grassy waters' to view the trees, plant life, and ecology. Trained volunteers frequent the walk at strategic points, often pointing out creatures one might otherwise miss. The sanctuary is world famous for the large breeding colony of the increasingly endangered wood stork, but hawks, owls, woodland birds, alligators, wading birds, and mosquitos may also be found there. Covered limbs and repellant are the answer for the latter, and luckily mosquito fish are also prolific in the swamp to feast on the larvae.

## Lake Okeechobee

In the middle of southern Florida is Lake Okeechobee. South and east of the lake is sugar country, with tall smokestacks of the sugar processing plants punctuating the miles of cane. North of Okeechobee is primarily rural farming and cattle country. Chains of smaller lakes lead past Sebring to Orlando and beyond to the Florida Border. Lake Okeechobee itself is a fisherman's paradise, but the scenery offers little for the tourist. The Herbert Hoover Dike surrounds the southern half of the lake, and the few vista points show a large body of water leading to a gently rounded horizon. The main points of interest are along Highway 27 to the west, while the best vantage point is Port Mayaca, on the eastern edge.

**Sebring** is world famous for the gruelling International Grand Prix Sports Car 12-hour Endurance Race held each year in mid-March. **Gatorland** is off Highway 27 to the south, with some of the largest alligators in captivity, although these days alligators can be spotted in the wild, for free. However, also on Highway 27 is the unique **Cypress Knee Museum**. Lining the roadside are the unusual tree signs which Tom Gaskins erected to catch the tourist's eye. A typical messages is, 'LADY IF HE WONT STOP HIT HIM ON HEAD WITH SHOE.' In the gnarled shape of a cypress knee, which aerates oxygen-starved roots, Tom could see presidents, movie stars, and a lifetime calling. His museum is a collection of unusual shapes, but he has also preserved wetlands which, without him, would have disappeared.

Between Sebring and Avon Park is **Highland Hammock State Park**, one of the largest natural hammocks in Florida, which was preserved long before the state had a park system. The main attraction is the eight short nature trails accessible from the three mile (5km) loop road. Not everyone walks each trail, but they can be combined via the loop road into a very pleasant 5 mile (8km) walk through the hammocks and cypress swamp. Bird and animal life abound under a palm and laurel oak canopy. Animals likely to be spotted include white-tailed deer, the gaudy but shy pileated wood-pecker, armadillo and, along the Little Charley Bowlegs Creek, turtles, otter, and alligators. Two sections of the park once cultivated oranges, and both orange and grapefruit trees grow heavy with citrus. Highland Hammocks is an excellent diversion from the bustle of Orlando or Tampa; a place to camp under the stars; to spot deer on a ranger guided trolley tour; or just to have a barbecue or picnic surrounded by woodlands.

## Additional Information

### Visitor Information

Greater Miami Convention and
    Visitors Bureau
701 Brickell Avenue, Suite 2700
Miami FL 33131
☎ 305-539-3000

Naples Area Chamber of Commerce
1700 North Tamiami Trail
Naples FL 33940
☎ 813-262-6141

### Local Events

*Late July*
Miccosukee Music & Crafts Festival
Miccosukee Indian Village

*Late Dec*
Miccosukee Indian Arts Festival
Miccosukee Indian Village

## Local, State & National Parks

*Big Cypress National Preserve*
Star Route Box 110 (US 41)
Ochopee FL 33943
☎ 813-695-2000 (Oasis 813-695-4111)
Open: 9am-4.30pm Mon-Fri, free.
Information at Oasis Ranger
Station, ₫

*Collier-Seminole State Park*
Route 4, Box 848 (Route 634)
Naples FL 33961
☎ 813-394-3397
Open: 8am-sunset. Canoe rental,
picnic, hike, camp, fort, ₫

*Corkscrew Swamp Sanctuary*
Route 6, 1875A (Route 846)
Naples FL 33964
☎ 813-657-3771
Open: 9am-5pm. Boardwalk, gifts,
self-guided tour, ₫

*Everglades National Park*
PO Box 279
Homestead FL 33030
☎ 305-247-6211
(Shark Valley 305-221-8455)
Main gate open 24hrs
Visitor center, gifts, walks, tours,
canoe & boat rental, ₫

*Highlands Hammock State Park*
5931 Hammock Road (Route 634)
Sebring FL 33872
☎ 813-385-0011
Open: 8am-sunset. Walks, picnic,
interpretive center, camp, ₫

*Chekika State Recreation Area*
PO Box 1313 (North on Route 997)
Homestead FL 33030
☎ 305-252-4438
Open: 8am-sunset. East Everglades
habitat, picnic, swim, camp, ₫

## Tourist Attractions

*Miccosukee Indian Village & Airboat Rides*
PO Box 440021 (US 41 Mile Marker 70)
Miami FL 33144
☎ 305-223-8380/8388
Open: 9am-5pm. Indian village,
gifts, airboat rides, restaurant

*Tom Gaskins Cypress Knee Museum*
PO Box 95 (US 27)
Palmdale FL 33944
☎ 813-675-2951
Open: 8am 'until closed'
Museum, walk, gifts, tour

## Tours and Transportation

*Eden of the Everglades*
Route 29
Everglades City FL 33929
☎ 813-695-2800 or 800-432-3367
Open: 10am-5pm. Boat tour, mini-
zoo, gifts, nature walks

*Everglades National Park Boat Tours*
PO Box 119
(Route 29, Chokoloskee Causeway)
Everglades City FL 33928
☎ 813-695-2591 or 800-445-7724
Open: 8.30am-5pm, cruise times
vary
Boat tours, canoe rental, gifts,
ranger station, ₫

*Wooten's Everglades Airboat Tours*
US 41
Ochopee FL 33943
☎ 813-695-2781
Hours vary
Airboat tours, swamp buggy,
alligator farm, gifts, snack bar

## Accommodation

Flamingo Lodge, Marina and
    Outpost Resort
Box 428
(Route 9336 from Homestead)
Flamingo FL 33030
☎ 305-253-2241 or 813-695-3101
Open: year-round, with full
facilities Nov to Apr
Cabins, rooms, restaurant (winter),
snacks, pool, gifts, canoe/boat
rental, tours, ₫

# 4

# *TAMPA*

# *AND THE GULF COAST*

Today a city undergoing phenomenal growth, **Tampa** has been a gateway to Florida ever since Ponce De Leon, Navarez, and De Soto sailed into Tampa Bay. But it was Henry Plant's railway that really sparked off Tampa's development, some three centuries later. Vast deposits of phosphates were discovered inland from Tampa, and the mining and shipping industries helped make Tampa one of the busiest ports and commercial centres in Florida. Tampa has no major beaches, but is still a busy tourist centre, studded with resorts, golf courses, with a fantastic coastline on its doorstep.

**Tampa International Airport** is considered to be America's finest, and it's use of people-movers has been extended to a new parking complex holding 7,000 vehicles. International and domestic arrival facilities are excellent, including hotel hotlines, free shuttles, and duplicated car rental kiosks.

Public transportation in and around Tampa is primarily by the HART Line (Hillsborough Area Regional Transit). Marion Street in downtown Tampa is the main terminus, with connections through the city and Hillsborough County. The Convention and Visitors Association's welcome/information centre on 111 Madison Street helps find hotels, golf courses, restaurants, and places of interest.

❋ **Busch Gardens, The Dark Continent** is the undisputed king of Florida's gulf coast attractions. Africa is the theme for this park which combines state-of-the-art thrill rides with the fourth largest zoo in America. There are eight themed areas within the park, many of which host entertainment throughout the day. As the world's largest brewer, they offer samples to those over 21 years old.

Through the main entrance to the gardens is Morocco, first of the park's themes. Visitors are welcomed by the Mystic Sheiks of Morocco Marching Band and some equally fancy Moorish tile work. The Moroccan Palace Theater rather surprisingly hosts the 'Around the

## Busch Gardens Tips

Entrance queues build rapidly just before opening time, so arrive early or wait until later. Protect cameras with a fold-up waterproof. Wear light, casual clothing, and be especially careful to protect shoulders, knees, and nose against sunburn. Height restrictions apply on the fastest rides, but there are many alternative rides just for younger children. Those just above the minimum height of 42in (107cm) may have to be accompanied on the faster rides. Most shows start several hours after the park opens and finish before closing. Busch provide a very handy show schedule and a park map upon entry to help plan the (very full) day's activities. Those planning to see other Busch attractions, such as Sea World, Cypress Gardens, or the nearby **Adventure Island** water park should purchase combination tickets and thereby save on entrance fees. The water park is open from March to October, and children under 8 years old must be accompanied by an adult.

World on Ice' revue. Right from Morocco is the Serengeti, a 60-acre natural environment for plains animals. The free-ranging 'wildlife' includes giraffes, gazelles, impala, camels, rhinoceros, and hippos. A skyway goes over the area, but some of the best viewing is from the suspended monorail or the balcony at Crown Colony.

Nairobi is often skipped by teenagers anxious to reach the rides quickly, but time in this zoo-themed section is worthwhile. Reptiles and fish are out in the sunlight but at the Nocturnal Mountain the creatures of darkness become active. A firm favourite with children is the Animal Nursery, where the public have excellent views of infant gazelle, lions, pot-bellied pigs, and parrots.

Timbuktu is just beyond the elephant enclosure. This remote desert outpost has some remarkably modern entertainment, including the Scorpion, a rollercoaster ride with a sting, and plenty of rides for younger children . In keeping with the main Busch activity of brewing, the Festhaus offers a family *Oktoberfest* atmosphere, with German-style food and entertainment. At the opposite end of Timbuktu is the highly entertaining Dolphin Theater.

In the Congo the rides become ever wilder. The children's rides give way to bumper cars and then the Python, a double corkscrew rollercoaster ride. Nearby is the Monstrous Mamba, with the tiger-infested Claw Island nearby. Cameras and other objects should be waterproofed before venturing onto the Congo River Rapids, a white-water rafting expedition. Busch Gardens sell rain ponchos for wet weather and splash-filled rides.

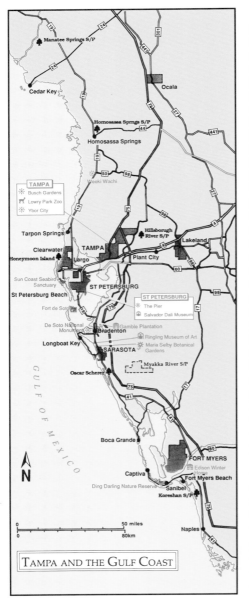

TAMPA AND THE GULF COAST

The next themed area is Stanleyville, named after the famous African explorer. Floating a 'dugout log' over the Stanley Falls is not *quite* as wet as the Congo Rapids. Soaked fun-lovers should head for the latest in water-bourne adventure, the Tanganyika Tidal Wave. The boat takes travellers through Orchid Canyon on a quiet ride — and then they climb. After a sharp drop comes the splash, which can catch innocent by-standers crossing the nearby bridge. For a photograph of the ride, cross the bridge quickly before the boat drops, and shoot from behind the splash guard. Stanleyville also houses the Zambezi Theatre, where variety acts are performed.

Beyond Stanleyville is a young children's activity area, followed by the Bird Gardens. In addition to the many birds on display there are hourly bird shows and a nearby Large Animal Display area

*Be prepared to get wet on the water rides at Busch Gardens*

*Lowry Park Zook has a unique Florida themed section*

with changing exhibits. The hospitality house also has shows, alternating between the rocking '60s and country music. Each guest aged 21 or over may try their complimentary two samples of beer.

The brewery tour commences with an escalator past the park's rescued American eagles. First one learns how Anheuser-Busch produce such good beer. The next section is fascinating, with bottles of beer filling and being capped so quickly one's head spins.

Beyond the brewery is Morocco and then Crown Colony. This American example of Victoriana is in front of the Clydesdale Hamlet, where the renowned Budweiser Clydesdales are kept. These magnificent horses were well suited to pulling heavy deliveries of beer before the internal-combustion engine took over, but today their function is more ceremonial.

In Crown Colony one also may sample the brewer's wares. The Colony is preferable to the hospitality house, as queues are shorter and the balcony provides a vista of the Serengeti. Upstairs is the new up-market Crown Colony House Restaurant.

Travellers can rarely see everything, but they should make some time for **Lowry Zoo**, which has a good selection of exotic mammals, birds, reptiles and the obligatory children's hands-on village. What makes Lowry Zoo special is their latest addition, the twelve-acre Florida Wildlife Center. Native animals and habitats vary from wetlands to dry prairie to coral reefs, linked by a boardwalk with access for wheelchairs or push chairs. Familiar Florida animals on display include alligator, myriad bird life, river otter, black bear, armadillo, and white-tailed deer. Less expected are the Bison and red wolves, which once roamed northern Florida and nearly became extinct. They have an American crocodile, and the cougars are part of a campaign to the save the Florida panther.

The star of the show is the endangered manatee, and here they have a specially-built manatee hospital, with a rescue unit, an operating theatre, three recovery tanks, and a research facility. The hospital is off-limits to visitors but the million-plus gallon aquarium complex is not. Spectators can view the myriad inhabitants of Florida's waterways, including the manatee. This water-bound cousin to the elephant swirls in the water like an astronaut in free-fall — clumsy in looks but graceful indeed. Surrounding the zoo is **Lowry Park**, which boasts shaded picnicking for the family, plus a free amusement park (rides extra) and safety village for the children.

Families will also enjoy the hands-on educational experience of the **Museum of Science and Industry**, situated across from the University of Southern Florida. Every hour a hurricane blows through the weather station, while the experiments in electricity, magnetism, and sound build a solid base for the section on communications. The grounds have three different walking trails which take the visitor through various Florida habitats.

At **Bobby's Seminole Indian Village** the main attraction is Seminole Bingo, where prizes reach tens of thousands of dollars and higher. This Vegas in miniature also has slot machines, high stakes bingo where a maximum of five play, a free hotel shuttle and a Sheraton hotel next door. Indian land is subject to its own special laws; it is rather like visiting another country without a passport. Hence the long queues of cars waiting to stock up on cigarettes at tax-free prices. For those interested in the Seminoles themselves, there is an Indian Trading Post with tours of their culture centre and village.

Historic **Ybor City** (pronounced Eebor) was founded as a haven for Cuban Refugees whose living conditions in their first sanctuary, Key West, grew intolerable. Soon Ybor was a bustling town, making hand-rolled cigars. It became the centre of American efforts to liberate Cuba from Spain, with cigar workers pledging their earnings and lives to the cause. The United States became embroiled, and when the Spanish-American war ended, the cigar industry thrived until hit by mechanization and the depression. Today Ybor City is part of Tampa, but its history is recalled by the **Ybor City State**  **Museum**, formerly a bakery. In addition they also provide a map of Ybor showing places of interest. **Ybor Square** is the town's first cigar factory, now a shopping mall. Amongst the antiques and boutiques is a store selling old postcards from around America. The Don Quijote restaurant serves authentic Cuban cuisine, including black beans and rice, while the quaint Italian grocery on 8th Avenue supplies Cuban sandwiches. The famous Columbia Restaurant on Ybor's 7th Street is now supplemented by another in the Market of Harbour Island. The fresh Cuban bread of Ybor comes from La Segunda Central Bakery on 15th Avenue, which provides tours on advance notification. Many Cubans remain around Ybor, and the city still remembers its heritage, but a melange of other inhabitants add to the local colour, including a strong New Age movement.

The 1987 **Tampa Bay Performing Arts Center** offers numerous shows and concerts in its Festival Hall, Playhouse, and the more intimate Jaeb Theater. Other productions are held at the Tampa Theater, a 1926 movie palace resembling a Moorish courtyard. Tampa Bay Hotel was taken over by the University of Tampa, but the south wing has been retained as the **Henry B. Plant Museum**. The  Moorish architecture and the spires of its minarets are unmistakable from the Performing Arts Center, and 1991 saw the building's 100th birthday celebrations.

Apart from the ubiquitous malls, Tampa has shopping at Harbour Island, a development south of the city centre adjacent to the new Convention Center. Harbour Island is a mix between touristy and trendy, and has good restaurants and nightlife, with the Harbour Island Hotel nearby. Mini-cruises of Tampa Bay and the Hillsborough River depart from Harbour Island, as does a water taxi service up to Lowry Park Zoo. Parking is available on the island, or pedestrians may take the PeopleMover across from the city. The shopping precincts at Harbour Island, Ybor Square, and turn-of-the-century Old Hyde Park Village also offer good people watching.

## St Petersburg

The 'Sun Capital of America' is Saint Petersburg's claim to fame, with a city record of 768 consecutive days of sunshine. So now St Petersburg and nearby Clearwater are surrounded by a sprawl of suburbs and resort communities which make tiny Pinellas the most densely populated county in Florida. The St Petersburg and Clearwater Beach environs are ideally suited to holidaymakers who want the calmer Gulf of Mexico beaches within a suburban resort atmosphere. Exciting Orlando and quieter, less-developed coastline are within the driver's reach, but access to connecting highways can be painfully slow. Travellers staying on or near the beach might wish to consider a tour bus to Walt Disney World or a boat trip to Tarpon Springs from Clearwater Marina — leaving the hassle to others.

❄ **The Pier** is *the* St Petersburg landmark with a long road running down its length, with plenty of parking on each side, and a five-storey inverted pyramid at the end. Inside are specialty shops, the aquarium, banqueting facilities, snack shops, a restaurant, an ocean-side bar, and the roof-top observation deck. The pier is a good place to watch people coming and going, do a bit of shopping, take in the informative and free aquarium, or even book a show at the Visitor Center. Outside one has an excellent view of the harbour: the St Petersburg Yacht Club is nearby, as is the Municipal Marina.

The St Petersburg Historical Society have a waterfront museum on the landward end of the pier. There are changing exhibits, and their displays are fresh and interesting. There are tours through the Haas Museum complex, with many period furnishings and the Lowe House exemplifying typical cracker architecture.

A short stroll from the pier is the **Museum of Fine Arts**, with ancient art, oriental, Renaissance, eighteenth- and twentiethth-century American and European works, as well as photography and a particularly well presented collection of Steuben Crystal. Guided

*St Petersburg Pier is as long as an airport runway*

tours give an introduction to the museum, while the gardens provide a peaceful respite from the heat and bustle of St Petersburg.

South of the pier is the **Salvador Dali Museum**, home to the largest collection of this renowned Spanish master's works. The industrialist A. Reynolds Morse and his wife, Eleanor Reese Morse, have long been fascinated by Dali and his art, and became close friends with this eccentric man. Their massive collection was donated to a specially created non-profit organization, whose mission is to ensure that others understand and better appreciate Dali. There are regular tours and especially interesting is coverage of Dali the child and his formative years. Entrance to the well-stocked gift shop, which has posters of many of the originals in the museum, is free.

Just inland from the Dali Museum is **Great Explorations**. This very modern hands-on science museum is great fun for children young and old. The various sections challenge both mind and body, such as their sense-enhancing maze called the touch tunnel. Explore galore is dedicated to the younger set, while the think tank develops problem-solving skills. The human physique is also put under scrutiny at the body shop, which concentrates on health. A special exhibit area changes regularly.

St Petersburg has a liberal sprinkling of parks, including several along the bay and many more inland. **Boyd Hill Nature Park** is some 216 acres of cycling (bring your own bike), picnicking, and has three miles (5km) of nature trails. The diverse ecosystems include lakeside, marshland, hardwood hammock, and dry scrubland. Nature programmes alter during the year, except the night hike which is always on the second Monday of the month.

Man has helped nature at the **Sunken Gardens**. Their gift shop is massive, well stocked, and must be circumnavigated to reach the gardens entrance. The actual gardens are awash with luxuriant tropical foliage, while the exotic birds appear along the walkways in their cages, the aviary, or at the obligatory bird show.

## St Petersburg Area Beaches

The beaches along this section of the Gulf of Mexico line a chain of barrier islands which nestle Pinellas County. The sand is white, the water topaz, and the sun is definitely hot. The level of development is high between St Petersburg and Clearwater Beaches, and these resort areas are geared for fun. Almost every conceivable water sport is available, with the level of activity ranging from a sedate cruise to parascending. Charter boats cater for salt-water fishing, snorkeling or diving, and a few specialize in throwing parties. At night the bars and discos are crammed with tanned locals and tourists.

The chain of islands which comprise the Pinellas County gulf beaches are linked together by Highways 699 and 183, effectively the same road. Beach access is reasonable, but lack of parking and slow traffic handicaps those arriving by car. Drivers should bring plenty of quarters for the parking meters if they are spending time on the beach. **Clearwater Beach** has more parking and is accessible from Tampa via Highway 60, which passes Tampa International Airport and crosses Old Tampa Bay over the long Courtney Campbell Causeway. Clearwater Beach *may* be the ideal base for a gulf coast vacation for those who want plenty to do: lots of people to watch; good beaches; a variety of shops and restaurants; a marina with charter boats; and a wide range of hotels, motels, and condominiums. The central location allows day-trips to Tampa and Orlando, perhaps even Spaceport USA. Driving hassle can be avoided by setting off *very* early in the morning, when it is cooler anyway, or booking a bus tour from your hotel.

South of Clearwater Beach is Sand Key Park, a useful parking spot when Clearwater becomes packed. Although there are innumerable excellent seafood restaurants along this stretch of coast, the queues are always longest at **Crabby Bills**. Crabby and family serve inexpensive, homestyle fresh oysters, onion rings, and combined lobster/shrimp/rib platters. The lightening-quick service ensures that the queue keeps moving. Crabby Bills is an experience, in the nicest sense of the word, but the one thing not on their menu is formal dining in a quiet atmosphere.

Families and animal lovers should not miss the **Suncoast Seabird**  **Sanctuary**. This hospital and home for less fortunate members of Florida's diverse bird life now treats about twenty injured birds daily. Visiting the sanctuary is free (donations welcomed) and highly educational. Silver-banded birds in the sanctuary are scheduled for release once they have gathered sufficient strength, while those unable to survive in the wild are offered a home for life. Of the 500 or so inhabitants, around 175 are brown pelican. In the wild they are endangered by loss of habitat and polluted fish, but most are victims of fishing hooks and lines. Anyone accidentally hooking a pelican should bring the bird to them — don't just cut the line! Many of the egrets, pelicans, gulls and herons perched on the aviary roof have been rescued and released, but they remember the sanctuary kindly and prefer to stay.

Just north of Treasure Island is a collection of designer shops lining a boardwalk in an area known as **John's Pass Village**. Unlike pastel Seaside, a shiny new resort complex on the Panhandle, John's Pass resembles a shanty fishing village, rusting tin roofs and all. A multi-storey parking lot is hidden in the complex, and many visitors spend the day on nearby beaches and the evening at the village.

South of the upmarket resorts of Treasure Island and St Petersburg Beach, on the Pinellas Bayway toll road, is the turnoff to **Fort De Soto Park**. Five keys connected by roads make up the park, a popular escape from busy Tampa and St Petersburg. The park was named after the Spanish-American War fortification built on the southern tip, a defence never used in earnest. Ponce De Leon visited the main island, Mullet Key, in 1513, but despite an attack by Indians he returned in 1521, and was mortally wounded. Another notable visitor was the brilliant Robert E. Lee, who recommended that the fortification be built on Mullet Key. Today's visitors are more intent on catching Pinellas County sunshine on the long beaches, swimming in the warm gulf waters, or enjoying shady picnic areas. Fort De Soto Park also has what should be the best camping spot in county. The campsites all have electricity and water, many have sewage hook-ups, the prices are not unreasonable, and the location is great. It would be heaven if they computerized their reservation system.

## South to Manatee County

Most travellers heading south from Tampa use Interstate 75, a quick route which does not suffer the strip development that chokes portions of Highway 41. The most scenic route from St Petersburg is undoubtedly via Interstate 275 over the **Sunshine Skyway**, which flies over Tampa Bay. A tugboat rammed the old bridge, so a skyscraper of a bridge replaced it, providing excellent views of the bay. The mouth of Tampa Bay is too wide for a single span, so only part of the drive is at high altitudes. At designated causeway pull-offs you may stop to fish or even lounge on a sandy beach. Keep an eye out for playful dolphins, which frequent the bay.

Across the bay is **Manatee County**. Interstate 75 hurries south towards Sarasota, Fort Myers, and Naples, with connections for Miami and the Everglades. Those with time may enjoy the scenic coastal route to Sarasota, with the first port of call the visitor centre at the junction of I-75 and Highway 301. They provide useful maps, tips on places to visit, and a complimentary cup of orange juice.

From the visitor centre follow Highway 301 west to the **Gamble Plantation State Historic Site**. This colonnaded antebellum home was constructed for Major Robert Gamble, who owned a 3,500 acre plantation and wanted a house which befitted his position. Sugar was the cash crop, although profitability was elusive in the early years because he invested heavily in land, slaves, the latest sugar-refining equipment and a fine home. Then, with success imminent,

*A rescued pelican at the Seacoast Seabird Sanctuary*

*The Ringling legacy, now the Florida State Art Museum, includes these classical-style gardens*

cheap imports caused sugar prices to plummet. The plantation was sold and the house eventually abandoned, but not before Judah P. Benjamin, the Confederate Secretary of State, hid there after the Civil War en route to safety in Britain. This saved it from destruction: the United Daughters of the Confederacy purchased the house because of its significance. They later donated their memorial to the State of Florida, who have an interpretive centre and provide tours.

The **South Florida Museum**, located across the Manatee River in Bradenton is as much an activity centre as a museum. Even their prehistoric Indian artifacts are arranged in coloured layers as in an archaeological dig. The planetarium and laser light shows take place regularly, and here is the oldest manatee born in captivity. Snooty is almost 50 years old, and at the time of writing was still going strong. Finally, one may visit the Spanish Courtyard to see a replica of the sixteenth-century church and home of Hernando De Soto.

Travel west on Manatee Avenue to learn how sharply the white-washed walls of De Soto's Spanish home contrasted with the palm-thatched *chickees* which he 'enjoyed' in Florida. During the cooler winter months the rangers at **De Soto National Monument** wear Spanish mail and re-enact the lifestyle of De Soto's troops. As well as cooking over an open fire they practice the crossbow and arquebus, an early type of musket. The interpretive centre is open all year-round, with rangers to answer questions and show a film of De Soto's ill-fated quest. The narrative, based upon the writings of a survivor, tells how De Soto pushed 500 men and himself beyond human endurance on a 4,000-mile journey through an unknown continent.

After surviving the De Soto expedition one may continue west on Manatee Avenue to Anna Maria Island. The road south follows the chain of barrier islands with mixed cottages, motels, and beach access. Halfway down Longboat Key is the Sarasota County boundary, and suddenly one has arrived.

# Sophisticated Sarasota

Sarasota has an air of being more cultured, of offering more refinement than a city of its age should. Although the transition from wilderness to self-styled cultural mecca was the effort of many, John and Mabel Ringling came to Sarasota during its formative years in the 1920s, and left the city its greatest legacy. Not only did they make their home in Sarasota, they made it the winter headquarters for their world famous circus, which had by then incorporated P.T. Barnum & Bailey's Greatest Show on Earth. The winter headquarters was later moved 20 miles south to Venice, where it is today, but the Ringlings stayed in Sarasota.

The **Ringling Museum Complex** was willed to the state of Florida, as was Ca'd'Zan, their palatial Venetian-style residence. They were enamoured with Europe, and they possessed one of America's largest collections of Baroque art, housed in a specially-built museum. The Ringling estate is now the State Art Museum of Florida. The grounds encompass 66 acres, and the canopy of trees gives the area a parklike feeling. The admission ticket is valid for all the three main buildings. The thirty rooms of Ca'd'Zan, or 'House of John', are decorated primarily in Venetian Gothic style, with magnificent views of Sarasota Bay. Wheelchair access is confined to the ground floor. The nearby Circus Galleries, converted from the estate's garages, house a collection of art and memorabilia from the heyday of the circus. Ringling amassed an incredible collection of Italian Baroque art, as well as works from Flemish and other European masters. The state has continued Ringling's efforts to broaden the collection, with the addition of American and contemporary works. Visitors in early March can enjoy the week-long festival of the Medieval Fair, when a fourteenth-century European village miraculously appears, complete with musicians, magicians, and maidens.

One structure within the Ringling Complex easily missed is the Old Asolo Theatre, which is not always open to the public. Inside the 1950s structure is an original Italian Baroque theatre which was reassembled in Sarasota to complement the art museum. The New Asolo Theater is larger, and has more facilities, but retains the European philosophy and atmosphere. The outside is akin to Mediterranean Revival, while the interior embellishments came from Scotland. Performing arts are also played at the Van Wezel Hall, giving visitors yet another chance to sample that Sarasota culture.

Across the road from the Ringling complex is **Bellm's Cars and Music of Yesterday**. Beyond the gift shop is a collection of working antique vending and fairground novelty machines. Two guided tours are provided and, depending upon arrival time, the first may be to the automobiles. Seemingly hundreds of cars in various states of repair form a long circle. The guide points out the major technological features which they pioneered, from battery powered cars to the first four-wheel steering. Bellm has one of the largest, and finest, collections of old phonograph players and music boxes to be found anywhere, from lamp stands that double as music boxes to a steam-powered orchestra. Virtually all are in working order, although some are too valuable to play every day. Nearby is the Lionel Train and Sea Shell Museum, which has a genuine railway car, antique model train sets, and shells from around the world.

Sarasota is at its tropical best at the **Marie Selby Botanical Gar-**

**dens**. Their collection of orchids and bromeliads is renowned, but the walk through the gardens' 11 bayside acres also includes natural Florida, a banyan grove, a tropical display house, an excellent display of cycads, and other interesting diversions, such as the Tropical Food Garden. The Selby house is now the gift shop, while their next-door neighbour's residence, the Payne's home, is the garden's Museum of Botany and the Arts.

Beaches and shopping are perhaps Sarasota's main pastimes. The barrier islands have some of the best beaches in Florida. For those who take the coastal route to Sarasota, relaxed Longboat Key connects northern Manatee County to Sarasota. Two keys which appear as one are Lido and St Armands Keys. The latter is best known for its fine shopping and dining congregated around **St Armands Circle**. The park in the centre was courtesy of John Ringling, and the sidewalk surrounding the park remembers those who made the circus the 'Greatest Show on Earth' in the Circus Ring of Fame.

Another place of interest is the **Mote Marine Aquarium**. Guides are on hand to answer questions about the marine life on display, and the aquarium shows many of the fish found in Florida's waters. The shark pool is popular and reflects the pioneering research here on 'the world's most efficient predators'.

South of Sarasota are more beaches on the barrier islands of Siesta and Casey Keys. **Venice** is famous for the petrified shark's teeth found on its beaches. Gasparilla Island has a state recreation area and the Boca Grande Lighthouse. No one road links all the islands, and coast huggers will find detours are inevitable. Many drivers just get onto US 41 and head south, while others remain on Interstate 75. In either event, no one should rush past without considering what may be Florida's finest state park, easily found by travelling east on Highway 72, which bisects US 41 and the Interstate from Siesta Key.

At 28,875 acres **Myakka River State Park** is Florida's largest state park. Facilities such as picnic tables and nature walks are supplemented with a an interpretive centre and two tours. The airboat ride around Upper Myakka Lake is popular year-round, with good opportunities for spotting the myriad waterfowl which live on and around the lake. Hawks, osprey, and bald eagles are common sightings, as are alligators. The sandhill crane, looking like a small emu with red paint on its head, is especially abundant during the winter bird-spotting season.

A tour train heads into the more remote sections of the park twice daily from mid-December to the end of May, with opportunity for seeing the wildlife of the varying habitats. Myakka has an extensive network of trails, 15 miles (24km) of which are designated for horses.

Walkers are in their element at Myakka, and rental cycles are available for use on designated trails. Canoe rentals are also available, with a choice between exploring the lake or river. The park's southern 7,500 acres are a preserve, although hiking and canoeing are allowed in limited numbers. For those who can spend longer, Myakka has two campgrounds and five rustic cabins.

## Fort Myers & Lee County

There was no railway to Fort Myers when Thomas Edison made it his winter residence in 1886. Other people were attracted to the area, and the young Henry Ford was so impressed by the industrialist-inventor that he bought the house next door. Today both homes, called the **Edison Ford Complex**, are open to the public. Apart from the Edison home, the property encompasses his workshops, laboratory, and extensive botanical gardens. Fort Myers then added a museum to house their massive collection of inventions and memorabilia. Later the Henry Ford home was added to the complex, which has reduced rates for visits to both houses. Viewing the homes and gardens is only by guided tours, which provide interesting background on the lives of the Edison and Ford families, and uses of certain plants within the gardens. If time permits only one home, then do not miss the Edison tour, which includes the museum and laboratories.

Additional information on the Edisons, Fords, and many other notable settlers is available at the **Fort Myers Historical Museum**. The passenger train reached Fort Myers in Thomas Edison's time and closed in 1971, leaving behind the perfect place for a history museum — the railway depot. Many artifacts are on display — the most massive of which is *Esperanza*, an 84ft-long, 101-ton private rail car. It was the largest ever built by Pullman, 17 ft longer than even George Pullman's own private car. The area's history encompasses the Calusa Indians, the Seminoles, cracker cattlemen, and Cyrus Reed Teed. He was leader of the Koreshan Unity, a religious community, who believe that the earth is a hollow sphere, and the world we know is on the inside, with the sun in the centre. Using equipment of his own devising, Koresh, as Mr Teed was known to his followers, 'proved' that his theories were correct. The Koreshan Unity advocated communal living with joint ownership of property and celibacy, but the movement declined after Teed's death. The remains of the original community are preserved and may be visited at **Koreshan State Historic Site**, which is south on US 41. Given that most of them were urbanites, they carved a pleasant niche for themselves in the Florida wilderness. In addition to the practical skills they learned, they brought with them civilization and culture, in the form of an orchestra, plays and pageants, and a printing press. The Koreshan Unity is still active, albeit not at their original settlement.

From Fort Myers city centre down McGregor Boulevard are the twin islands of **Sanibel** and **Captiva**. In the old days access was only by boat and the islands were refreshingly natural, which is how the residents wanted it. Since then the islands have suffered from development. The highly-contested toll bridge virtually wiped out the fishing industry, and today brings a flotilla of cars on sunny weekends. Sanibel shelling is renowned, and the influx of professional shellers had to be curbed by allowing a maximum of two live shells per day. Another natural attraction that draws crowds is the Ding Darling Wildlife Refuge. Their bird life in winter is amongst Florida's best, made even more popular because automobiles are allowed through the refuge. Residents get around by bicycle, the best way of enjoying the islands and avoiding traffic. Sanibel and Captiva are certainly not utterly spoilt, they are still relatively natural and pleasant — they just need a massive car park before the islands and a trolley service.

**Fort Myers Beach** has 7 miles of sand. The motels and resorts here are generally less exclusive and expensive than Sanibel, with plenty of T-shirt shops, restaurants, bars, and nightlife. Those with a motorhome should check out the Red Coconut RV Resort, as there are not many in Florida with a prime on-the-beach setting. One-night visits are allowed, although in winter many residents are semi-permanent, and caravans can be hired (three days minimum — monthly rates a speciality). Just before Fort Myers Beach is the marina, with sunset cruises on the *Eagle*, and innumerable boats available for charter. Several companies operate jet ski rentals around Fort Myers Beach.

Southern Fort Myers Beach is sprouting condominiums, while the next islands south have beaches with natural settings. **Lovers Key** is being developed, but only by the State Parks people, who will be adding toilets and similarly useful facilities. Until then, there is an access boardwalk and very little else — apart from nesting osprey, mangrove thickets, and an uncrowded beach. The next key south is the site of Carl Johnson Park, which has slightly more facilities, but is also a relatively undisturbed beach. These islands are not some great secret; they are just off the main highway. Delnor-Wiggins Pass State Recreation Area to the south also offers a natural beach atmosphere, but with extra facilities like a bird observation tower and changing rooms. Those taking the coastal route south might visit Koreshan on the way back north, or vice versa.

# Naples Niceties

Sarasota has its culture, Tallahassee its southern charm, and Miami a cosmopolitan atmosphere. Naples prides itself on a rather more nebulous quality — lifestyle. When determining which factors constitute a high standard of life, many cities substitute quantity for quality — the longest beaches; the most golf courses; 50 percent more shopping malls; the greatest population. You then spend half a day trying to park near a beach, only to find it is overcrowded; the shops all pander to the tastes of a bland majority; and next available slot at the golf/tennis court is the day after you return home. Like other cities, Naples offers the most beach, the best shopping, and the highest number of golf courses — but per person.

Lifestyle is not just having these facilities, but it makes a good start. Naples is right on the beach, and the planners have included plenty of convenient parking and access. The climate is balmy almost year-round, so the many trees and palms offering shade are very welcoming. Third Street is the newest, most exclusive shopping district. The parking behind it is free, but the parking attendants get agitated if visitors then slip off to the nearby Naples pier and beaches. Inland is Tin City, which harks back to Naples' days as a fishing village. Tour and charter boats run from the marina nowadays, while the shops, bars, and restaurants there have a relaxed, informal atmosphere. Between 3rd Street and Tin City is Fifth Avenue, the original shopping district.

The **Collier County Museum** has historical displays from the  times of the Calusa Indians to Barron Collier, developer of the Tamiami Trail. The **Collier Automotive Museum** was founded by  Barron's grandson Miles Collier. Miles' father and two uncles were keen sports car enthusiasts, and supported road racing in America. Miles has built the museum as a tribute to his family and their overriding passion — the sports-racing car, with exemplary exhibits worthy of an art gallery. The collection of Porche vehicles is considered America's finest, with a quality of display said to be better than at the Porsche factory museum. Each fascinating car is maintained in perfect running order, and the museum is the ideal place to get try a Grand Prix race car for size.

Another fine collection may be found at **Frannie's Teddy Bear**  **Museum**. Imported bears, special edition bears, designer bears, bears of note — all living in a specially-built museum. Virtually anything to do with teddies can be found there, even a library of books for those barely (or should it be bearly!) old enough to read.

Naples has its own Performing Arts Center, and the novelty of good food and productions at the **Naples Dinner Theater**. Of course a French chef helps, and the owners scour Broadway once or twice a year, but note that gentlemen should wear jackets, and those who arrive first, dine first.

Naples is also a handy gateway to the western half of the Everglades. The airboat, swamp buggy, and standard boat tours of Everglades City are only just around the corner. The Shark Valley entrance to Everglades National Park is not far, and is a leisurely day trip when combined with the Miccosukee Indian Village. The Audubon society's Corkscrew Swamp Sanctuary is just inland from Naples, and Collier-Seminole State Park is just to the south.

For nature in the heart of Naples do not miss **The Conservancy**, which has an excellent interpretive centre and walks, and demonstrate Naples' determination to remain a natural destination.

## North of Tampa

Several treasures of the coast are just north of the Tampa/St Petersburg/Clearwater metropolis. On Alternate US Highway 19 north of Clearwater are Honeymoon and Caladesi Island State Recreation Areas. Honeymoon Island is ideal for those not staying at a beach resort, as the nominal parking fees are lower than hungry parking meters. Caladesi Island is yet more remote — access is by private boat or ferry from Honeymoon Island or Clearwater Marina.

When the Key West sponging industry was blighted the Greek divers there found a new home at **Tarpon Springs**. Although the area has developed considerably since, the Greek atmosphere is still there, especially around the sponging docks. The Spongerama Exhibit Center is an interesting place to browse. There are Greek restaurants, and a few cafés providing Greek food at take-away prices. Several boat tours run from the docks, while those not wanting to drive from Clearwater can catch a tour boat from their marina. The sponging industry has gone through a recent revival, with Europe the major market. The modern sponge fleets go further and stay out longer than of old, but there is still a flurry of activity as boat loads of sponges are graded and auctioned at the dock. The beaches at Tarpon Springs and further north are nothing special, but Honeymoon and Caladesi Islands are only a short drive away. On 6 January the Greek Orthodox Church holds its Epiphany celebration, with a procession through the streets. Young men dive for a gold cross during the Greek Cross Ceremony, and the lad who retrieves  it is blessed with a year's good luck. The nearby Universalist Church on Grand Boulevard displays landscape panels by George Inness Jr,

*Sponging is still big business at Tarpon Springs* ⇒

whose ability to portray living greens and light was dubbed the Inness perspective.

To see manatees and other Florida animals, visit **Homosassa Springs Wildlife Park**, which has manatees on view 365 days a year. Due to declining manatee populations, those at Homosassa have been isolated from the rest of Florida's waters, for protection and studying. Homosassa is also a great place to spot other Florida animals, like alligators and crocodile, and fish spotting could not be easier from their floating observatory. **Weeki Wachee** has combined mermaids with another spring to bring underwater ballet to Florida tourists, and they provide regular shows, a river cruise, animal displays, and a large petting zoo.

**Cedar Key** was the Gulf Coast end of the first trans-Florida railway, long before the coming of Henry Plant and Henry Flagler. David Yulee had developed one of the first resorts at Fernandina Beach, and Cedar Key was in those days the deepest port near his sugar mills, so Yulee used his political contacts to have the railroad link the two. The Civil War intervened, and the tracks were pulled up, although both Highway 301 and Amtrak still detour inland from Jacksonville to Gainesville following the route of the old railway. At the Yulee Sugar Mill Ruins State Historic Site the mill never survived the transition from slave labour, while Cedar Key went into a time warp after the fishing industry declined. The Cedar Key of today is a relaxing detour from modern Florida, with the same quaint fishing village atmosphere and seafood restaurants one finds in New England, but with the sunshine and sub-tropical climate of Florida.

Before taking the inevitable detour into Central Florida, go to the **Manatee Springs State Park**. Boats large and small ply the Suwannee River, and their propellers slice through the underwater weeds which the manatee feeds upon. As an experiment the park made the river bend nearest the springs off limits to propeller-driven craft and the manatees have since multiplied. Of course they are not captive, like those protected at Homosassa, so they spread out in the summer. Naturally the park is open year-round, and they have many other activities, such as bird watching, picnicking, swimming in the springs, and sailing rental canoes on the Suwannee. But on cold wintery mornings, manatees can be found congregating just outside the springs, surfacing every few minutes or so. In the quiet of the park their deep breaths punctuate the stillness.

# Additional Information

## Visitor Information

Lee Country Visitor & Convention
  Bureau
2180 W First Street
Fort Myers FL 33901
☎ 813-335-2631 or 800-237-6444

Naples Area Chamber of Commerce
1700 North Tamiami Trail
Naples FL 33940
☎ 813-262-6141

Pinellas County Tourist Development
  Council
4625 East Bay Drive, Suite 109
Clearwater FL 34624
☎ 813-530-6452

Sarasota Convention & Visitors
  Bureau
655 North Tamiami Trail
Sarasota FL 34236
☎ 813-957-1877

Tampa/Hillsborough Convention
& Visitors Association
111 Madison Street, Suite 1010
Tampa FL 33602
☎ 813-223-1111 or 800-826-8358

## Local Events

*Jan (Greek Epiphany)*
Festival of the Epiphany
Tarpon Springs

*Late Jan, Early Feb*
Gasparilla Festival
Tampa

*Early-Mid Feb*
Edison Pageant of Light
Fort Myers

Florida State Fair
State Fairgrounds, Tampa

*Early March*
Medieval Fair
Sarasota

*Late March, early April*
Festival of the States
St Petersburg

De Soto Celebration
Bradenton

*Mid April*
Dunedin Highland Games &
  Scottish Festival
Dunedin

*Late April, early May*
Fun 'n Sun Festival
Clearwater

*Late Sep, early Oct*
St Petersburg Beachfest
St Petersburg

*Late Oct*
John's Pass Seafood Festival
Madeira Beach

*Late Oct, early Nov*
St Petersburg Grand Prix Power-
  boat Race
St Petersburg

## Places of Interest

**Bradenton**
*DeSoto National Monument*
75th St NW
FL 34209-0097
☎ 813-792-0458
Open: 8am-5.30pm, free
Visitor centre, gifts, museum, &

*South Florida Museum*
201 10th St West
FL 34205
☎ 813-746-4132
Open: 10am-5pm Tue-Sat,
1pm-5pm Sun
History museum, planetarium,
gifts, replica De Soto home, &

## Brooksville
*Weeki Wachee*
PO Box 97 (Jct US 19 & Route 50)
FL 34605-0097
☎ 904-596-2062
Open: 9am-late, shows from 11am-5pm
Mermaid & bird shows, boat ride, petting zoo, food, gifts

## Chiefland
*Manatee Springs State Park*
Route 2, Box 617 (Route 320 off US 19 & 98)
FL 32626
☎ 904-493-4288
Open: 8am-sunset
Swim, picnic, canoe rental, camp, &

## Dunedin
*Honeymoon Island State Recreation Area*
No 1 Causeway Blvd
FL 34698
☎ 813-734-4255
Open: 8am-sunset
Beach, picnic, changing, &

## Ellenton
*Gamble Plantation State Historic Site*
3708 Patten Ave
FL 34222
☎ 813-722-1017
Open: 8am-sunset (museum 9am-4pm)
Admission fee for tour
Interpretive center, house tours, picnic

## Estero
*Koreshan State Historic Site*
PO Box 7 (US 41)
FL 33928
☎ 813-922-0311
Open: 8am-Sunset, tours vary
Historic village, self-guided tours, camp, picnic, &

## Fort Myers
*Edison-Ford Winter Homes*
2350 McGregor Blvd
FL 33901
☎ 813-334-7419
Open: 9am-4pm Mon-Sat, 12.30pm-4pm Sun
Guided tour of homes & gardens, museum, gifts, &

*Fort Myers Historical Museum*
2300 Peck St
FL 33901
☎ 13-332-5955
Open: 9am-4.30pm Mon-Fri, 1pm-5pm Sun
Gifts, Pullman car, &

## Homosassa
*Homosassa Springs State Wildlife Park*
9225 W Fishbowl Drive
FL 32646
☎ 904-628-5343
Open: 9am-5pm
Underwater viewing of springs, animals including manatees, gifts, &

## Indian Shores
*Suncoast Seabird Sanctuary*
18328 Gulf Blvd
FL 34635
☎ 813-391-6211
Open: 9am-sunset, free
Bird hospital, gifts, guided tours by appointment, &

## Madeira Beach
*John's Pass Village & Boardwalk*
12921 Gulf Blvd East
FL 33708
☎ 813-397-7242
Galleries, restaurants, boutiques, and waterfront boardwalk

**Naples**
*Collier Automotive Museum*
2500 Horseshoe Drive
FL 33942
☎ 813-643-5252
Open: 10am-6pm Fri, Sat, Sun
Vintage and sports-racing cars,
tours, &

**Osprey**
*Oscar Sherer State Recreational Area*
1483 S Tamiami Trail (US 41)
FL 33229
☎ 813-966-3154
Open: 8am-sunset
Swim, picnic, canoe rental, camp, &

**St Petersburg**
*Fort DeSoto Park*
South of Route 682, Pinellas Byway
FL 33701
☎ 813-866-2484
Open: Dawn-sunset, free
Beach, picnic, fort, walks, camp,
store, concessions,&

*Great Explorations*
1120 Fourth Street South
FL 33701
☎ 813-821-8885
Open: 10am-5pm Mon-Sat,
noon-5pm Sun
Hands-on learning, gifts, &

*Museum of Fine Arts*
255 Beach Drive NE
FL 33701
☎ 813-896-2667
Open: 10am-5pm Tue-Sat,
1pm-5pm Sun
Gifts, tours (multilingual by
appointment), &

*The Pier*
800 Second Ave NE
FL 33701
☎ 813-821-6164
Open: 10am-9pm, free
Shops, aquarium, restaurant,
observation deck, mini golf, fish,
info, &

*Saint Petersburg Historical Museum*
335 Second Ave NE
FL 33701
☎ 813-894-1052
Open: 10am-5pm Mon-Sat,
1pm-5pm Sun

*Salvador Dali Museum*
1000 Third St South
FL 33701
☎ 813-823-3767
Open: 10am-5pm Tue-Sat,
noon-5pm Sun
Tours, gifts, &

**Sanibel**
*Ding Darling National Wildlife
    Refuge*
1 Wildlife Drive
FL 33957
☎ 813-472-1100
Check — closed certain days due to
human impact
Gifts, visitor centre, tour via car or
cycle, &

**Sarasota**
*Bellm's Cars and Music of Yesterday*
5500 N Tamiami Trail
FL 34243
☎ 813-335-6228
Open: 8.30am-6pm Mon-Sat,
9.30am-6pm Sun
Vintage cars, music boxes, arcade,
gifts, tours, &

*Marie Selby Botanical Gardens*
811 S Palm Ave
FL 34236
☎ 813-366-5730
Open: 10am-5pm
SG tour, themed areas, gifts, plant
shop, &

*Myakka River State Park*
13207 State Rd 72
FL 34241-9542
☎ 813-924-1027
Open: 8am-sunset
Airboat & tram tours, hike, rental
canoes, store & snacks, camp, &

*Ringling Museum Complex*
PO Box 1838 (North on US 41)
FL 33578
☎ 813-355-5101
Open:10am-6pm, 10am-10pm Thur
Art museum, Ringling home, circus
museum, restaurant, gifts, &

**Tampa**
*Busch Gardens The Dark Continent*
3000 Busch Blvd
FL 33674
☎ 813-971-8282
Open: 9.30am-6pm extended
summer & holidays
Zoo, rides, restaurants & snacks,
gifts, brewery tour, &

*Harbor Island Shops*
601 South Harbor Island Blvd
FL 33602
☎ 813-228-7807
Entertainment, shops, restaurants,
boat cruises, &

*Henry B. Plant Museum*
401 W Kennedy Blvd
FL 33602
☎ 813-253-3333
Open: 10am-4pm Tue-Sat

*Lowry Park Zoo*
7530 N Blvd
FL 33604
☎ 813-935-8552
Open: 9.30am-5pm
Exotic & Florida sections, gifts,
restaurant & snacks, &

*Museum of Science & Industry*
4801 East Fowler Ave
FL 33617
☎813-985-5531
Open: 10am-4:30pm
Hands-on learning, gifts, food,
tours, &

*Ybor City State Museum*
1818 9th Ave
FL 33605
☎ 813-247-6323
Open: 9am-noon and 1pm-5pm
Tue-Sat
Tour, &

**Tarpon Springs**
*St Nicholas Greek Orthodox Cathedral*
30 North Pinellas Ave
FL 34689
☎ 813-937-3540
Free

*Spongeorama Exhibit Center*
510 Dodecanese Blvd
FL 34689
☎ 813-942-3771
Open: 10am-6pm
Museum & shops free
Theatre, restaurant & snacks, boat
tours, &

**Thonotosassa**
*Hillsborough River State Park*
15402 US 301 North
FL 33592
☎ 813-986-1020
Open: 8am-sunset
Historic fort, hike, picnic, swim,
canoe rental, camp, &

# 5

# *ORLANDO:*

# *THE HEART OF FLORIDA*

Between Orlando, Walt Disney World, and Kissimmee is the 'Tourist Triangle'. Walt Disney World is about 22 miles (35km) southwest of downtown Orlando on Interstate 4, which forms the long diagonal of the Tourist Triangle. Halfway between the two are Sea World, Universal Studios, Wet N' Wild, with shopping, dining, and entertainment around International Drive. Kissimmee is 12 miles (19km) east of Walt Disney World on Highway 192, a multiple lane road packed with motels, dining extravaganzas, amusement parks, and anything else the millions of holidaymakers can and do desire. From Kissimmee north on combined Highways 17/92 and 441 (really only one road at that point) to Orlando is about 18 miles (29km), with fewer attractions and traffic than US Highway 192.

Beyond the triangle is the rest of Florida. Interstate 4 starts near Busch Gardens in Tampa, just a short drive from the Gulf of Mexico coast. At the northeastern end is Daytona Beach and the Atlantic Ocean. The Florida Turnpike runs almost perpendicular to I-4, linking routes from the Florida Panhandle through the triangle and then southwest to Miami, with connections to the Florida Keys and Everglades. The Bee Line Expressway goes east from Interstate 4, past Orlando International Airport, to Cocoa Beach and Kennedy Space Center's Spaceport USA.

Arrivals to Orlando International Airport will find virtually every amenity. Public transport to the myriad motels is nothing special — there are too many resorts over too great a distance — so alternatives may be preferable. Package holidays should have transportation to the hotel arranged, but there are numerous companies willing to ferry people to major theme parks and shopping areas around Orlando. Some motels offer free shuttles to the theme parks, so when booking check if free transportation is included. Car rental in Florida is among the least expensive in America, especially by the week.

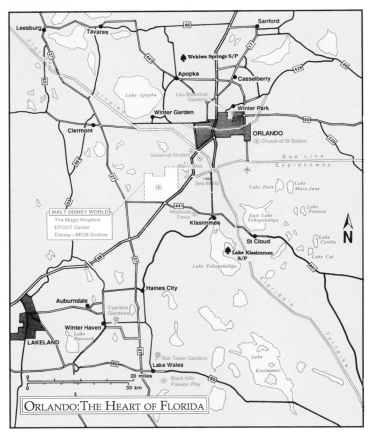

ORLANDO: THE HEART OF FLORIDA

The countryside north of Orlando is full of forests, springs, thoroughbred stud farms, and the mighty Saint Johns River. To the south from Kissimmee is orange and cattle country, with gardens thrown in. East and west are the coasts, while around and throughout the Tourist Triangle are central Florida's hundreds of lakes.

## Walt Disney World Resort

At last count there were some twenty resort hotels in Walt Disney World, with land, water, and/or monorail transportation into the

*Every.night is New Year's Eve at Pleasure Island* ⇒

themed parks. Among the options are Disney's Yacht and Beach Club Resorts, the Walt Disney World Swan and Walt Disney World Dolphin, and the affordable Disney's Caribbean Beach Resort, all of which are 'EPCOT Resorts'. Then there is Disney's Grand Floridian Beach Resort, Disney's Contemporary Resort, the quieter Disney Inn, the entertaining Disney's Polynesian Resort, and Disney's Fort Wilderness Resort and Campground; all these are 'Magic Kingdom Resorts'. The remaining are the Walt Disney World Village Hotels, which also have transportation to the theme parks and access to reservation services. Entertainment is strung throughout the resort hotel network, although guests should not forget the theme parks.

Also at the Walt Disney World Resort are three championship golf courses, numerous tennis courts, as well as hiking, biking, jogging, and horse riding trails. The marinas are packed with boats of varying sizes, and many resorts have beaches as well as swimming pools.

Even those who choose not to stay at a Walt Disney World Resort may wish to cool off at River Country, with two flume rides, rapids, and swimming. The adventurous may prefer to experience **Typhoon Lagoon**, where man-made waves are big enough to body surf on, and the fastest of the many flumes hits 30mph. Shoppers can head for **Disney Village Marketplace**, for Disney and Florida memorabilia. Last, but certainly not least, is **Pleasure Island**, where every night is New Year's Eve. Six clubs offer a choice of music and entertainment, with fireworks and a street party afterwards. The minimum age to be served alcohol in Florida is 21, and one must be 18 or older to visit a Pleasure Island club unless accompanied by an adult. Cover charges and entrance age restrictions do not apply in the restaurants or at the ten-theatre cinema.

## ❋ The Magic Kingdom

Names are important within Walt Disney World, as anyone who mentions Disneyland will discover. 'Oh, you mean the Magic Kingdom,' is the typical reply. The **Magic Kingdom** *is* the old Disney Magic, a mixture of Cinderella Castle, Mickey Mouse, the Wild West, Mark Twain, Tinker Bell and Dumbo.

The Magic Kingdom is a ferry boat or monorail ride from the main entrance car park off Interstate 4 and Highway 192. Beyond the entrance is **Main Street USA**, America as it should have been. For first timers this is an excellent introduction to the Magic Kingdom. The street is a mixture of shops, eateries, pop-up Disney characters, and good old-fashioned fun. Entertainment schedules for the day, such as the Disney Character Hit Parade, can be picked up at City Hall. The Walt Disney World Railroad steams from Main Street,

# Walt Disney Theme Parks Tips

The gates of each theme park officially open at 9o'clock in the morning, but those arriving by car and needing to purchase tickets may wish to arrive earlier. When arriving by car, especially in an unfamiliar rental car, it is advisable to write down the parking lot, row, and position, as an all-night search might be the alternative. Walt Disney World produces the very comprehensive *Disabled Guests Guide Book*, which they are happy to send to visitors. It outlines major rides and facilities throughout Walt Disney World. Rental wheelchairs and motorized convenience vehicles are available on a first-come basis, and many of the attractions, shows, and rides are accessible to those in non-motorized wheelchairs. However, it is essential that those who require assistance onto the other rides visit with a trained and physically able companion, as Walt Disney attractions personnel are not permitted to assist people on and off the rides. Having said that, the Disney personnel are experts at ensuring the transitions are smooth. Food may not be brought into the parks, but there are innumerable restaurants and snack bars. Picnic lunches outside the theme park are an option, but always have your hand stamped upon exit and keep your ticket or re-entry will be expensive.

There are three ticket options. The One Day Pass is valid for one day at one theme park. To visit all three parks one must buy three One Day Passes, or the slightly more expensive Four Day Pass. The latter also allows travel over the Walt Disney World transportation network. When going from one theme park to another, remember to ask for a hand stamp before leaving the first park. Holders of the Five Day Pass have similar privileges as those with Four Day Passes. All unused One Day Passes and remaining days on the longer passes may be saved for your next visit to Walt Disney World.

circumnavigating the Magic Kingdom and stopping at points of interest. The street itself is easily walked or toured by the many horse-drawn trolleys, jitneys, omnibuses and other vehicles. One easily missed attraction which should be included, perhaps in the evening when the entrance crowds are less, is the Walt Disney Story.

Most visitors prefer to see the Magic Kingdom clockwise, which makes **Adventureland** the next port of call. The gigantic replica of the Swiss Family Treehouse is fun for children and agile adults, while the more sedentary Jungle Cruise is a very relaxed introduction to the 'wilds' of Africa. One of the first examples of Disney's imaginative world of Audio-Animatronics awaits the visitor to the

Tiki Room (Tropical Serenade), where the Polynesian decor awakens into a colourful musical revue. Then on to one of the most popular Audio-Animatronics adventures — the boat ride down to the Pirates of the Caribbean. The imagination and attention to detail is pure Disney, so enjoy the humorous cameos of life as a pirate.

Next is **Frontierland**, a look at America's West. In addition to the main attractions is the occasional bank robbery shoot-out, which the sheriff invariably wins. The Disney Character Hit Parade is best seen from Frontierland, with all the favourite characters waving from the floats as they pass.

Big Thunder Mountain Railroad is a roller coaster ride through the days of the gold rush. Height restrictions apply to young prospectors and queues are longest in the morning, so it may pay to return later.

Tom Sawyer Island is a relaxing respite from the crowds, but Disneyophiles make a bee-line for the Audio-Animatronics high jinks of the Country Bear Jamboree. This foot-stompin' country revue is delivered by a whole gang of larger than life bears. The shows alter seasonally, with Christmas favourites sung from Thanksgiving. Each performance is just like living inside a Disney Cartoon. The Diamond Horseshoe Jamboree is reminiscent of another, even wilder West, but reservations to this popular show with *real* dancing girls should be made as early as possible on Main Street.

**Liberty Square** remembers the early days, when the thirteen British colonies suddenly awakened into a nation. The importance of water-bourne transportation is reflected by the Mike Fink Keelboats, while Liberty Square harkens to the glorious days of the Mississippi Riverboat. Within the hallowed Hall of Presidentsis a very patriotic view of early American history, supplemented with an animatronics cast of every President from George Washington to George Bush. Star of the show is Abraham Lincoln, but watch the other presidents, too, as they fidget or nod their heads to his speech.

Beyond the Liberty Square Riverboat, a genuine steam-driven stern-wheeler, lurks a spectre of doom at the Haunted Mansion. The spooktacular effects should not be missed, and fright is tempered with delight at the clever technology which created them. Repeat visits are necessary to fully appreciate the humour and level of detail.

No less than twelve attractions await the youngster in **Fantasyland**, although this area's popularity can reduce parents to tears. Even the least ride can command a long queue at mid-day, so those with children may wish to arrive here first or leave it until last. Cinderella Castle is popular with younger children, as is a quick spin on the Merry-Go-Round (Cinderella's Golden Carrousel). Family entertainment, such as a comical version of 'Sword in the Stone', regularly takes place in front of the castle.

Next is **Mickey's Starland** — born from our favourite mouse's sixtieth birthday celebration. Mickey's House is full of memorabilia, while his back door leads to a fun-filled show. Guests wishing to

*The Temple of Heaven blesses the EPCOT skyline*
(© The Walt Disney Company)

photograph children or friends with this most celebrated rodent should check the show times and catch Mickey in his Dressing Room before a show empties.

At **Tomorrowland** Space Mountain towers over the other rides and attractions. Those passing the health, height, and age restrictions (mainly good heart, back, and over 7 years old), ride a tight, fast rollercoaster through a dark cavern, with only comets and stars for a background. The WEDway PeopleMover takes a tour around Tomorrowland, to give an overview of the other attractions in this section of the Magic Kingdom. The Carousel of Progress highlights the progress which electricity has enabled since 'grandma and grandpa's day'. At the Tomorrowland Theatre the whole Disney cast can be seen and heard in a lively song and dance show.

During summer months and certain holidays the Magic Kingdom hours are extended as late as midnight. During these periods additional events are staged, such as the Main Street Electrical Parade and the Fantasy in the Sky Fireworks Display. Over-the-counter food is available throughout the Magic Kingdom, but for a sit-down meal try Tony's Town Square Restaurant, the Plaza Restaurant, King Stefan's Banquet Hall, Liberty Tree Tavern, or the Crystal Palace Buffeteria. An evening meal at Liberty Tree and King Stefan's may be booked during the day at their respective doors.

## ✳ EPCOT Center

Walt Disney's most grand, imaginative vision must have been his Experimental Prototype Community of Tomorrow. EPCOT for short, his concept was a revolutionary domed-city of the future, where 20,000 people could live, freed from the afflictions of progress: pollution, overpopulation, crime, and stress. EPCOT was to be a showcase to the rest of the world, proving that the human race could live in harmony, and imaginative usage of technology was the key. Although Walt Disney died in 1966, his dream lived on, albeit altered by the processes required to convert the concept into reality.

The two main thrusts of Disney's idea, the city of the future and the world living in harmony, became the twin pillars of EPCOT. Future World is a showplace of technology, which focuses on discovery and scientific achievement in nine themed areas. World Showcase presents the essence of selected nations of our world, including their architecture, art, cuisine, music, entertainment, and crafts. Together they make a fascinating day or two of sightseeing.

Those wishing to sample a particular country's cuisine should book early, preferably at a WorldKey terminal under Spaceship Earth at Earth Station. Reservations may also be made at the desired restaurant, but that may be fully booked by WorldKey terminal users before those walking reach it. Guests at any Walt Disney World Resort Hotel get priority over day visitors, and can book in advance.

Beyond the entrance plaza is the 180ft-high geosphere of Spaceship Earth, the unmistakable symbol of EPCOT. Most make a beeline for this gigantic beacon of technology, so it is often better to head for the more rearward themed areas of Future World or directly into World Showcase and visit Spaceship Earth later. This guide must logically deal first with Future World, but the visitor need not.

Although **Future World** is a showcase of technology, many of the techniques of people management it uses were perfected over the years at Disneyland. The endlessly moving chair of **Spaceship Earth** is an excellent example, ensuring a constant flow of guests past the carefully timed and presented images. Communications from the earliest cave drawings to modern satellite technology is the theme, and visitors are then 'projected' into space for an astronaut-eye view of the spaceship we call home.

**Earth Station**, below and behind Spaceship Earth, is the home base for the WorldKey Information Service. Apart from booking restaurants one may ask for information about current happenings in EPCOT and throughout the Walt Disney World Resort. Nearby are **CommuniCore East and West**, which host exhibits of ever-changing technology. Communicore East presents Backstage Magic, where the computers which automate the Vacation Kingdom are put through their paces. CommuniCore West looks at the very latest in communications and robotics, and highlights developments too new to include in Spaceship Earth.

Outside the above core at EPCOT are seven major themes which will affect our lives today and in the future. The first is the **Universe of Energy**, a 45-minute moving presentation of our sources of energy, and the options currently being explored. Next comes the **Wonders of Life**, which looks at our inner world. Those who love fast paced action head for Body Wars, where microminiaturized guests are injected into a patient's bloodstream on what *should* be a routine mission. The special effects are made possible through specially programmed space-age simulators, thus age and health restrictions apply on this turbulent 'ride'. The Wonders of Life theme area also has plenty of gentler ways of examining the body. Cranium Command is a light-hearted trip through a 12-year-old's brain, while one of Disney's favourite characters is the host of Goofy About Health. The more serious might prefer the Lifestyle Review, where a computer analyzes one's lifestyle and suggests health related improvements. After exploring the Frontiers of Medicine visitors can have their golf swing examined, or interactively discover how we sense the world about us. Needless to say, the 'snacks' served in Pure and Simple are good and healthy.

Habitats of the future is the theme of **Horizons**: beneath the ocean, a desert farm, space, and urban life. Then it's the **World of Motion**, a sometimes light-hearted look at transportation since the invention of the wheel. Certainly one should never underestimate the importance of the automobile in America, where people eat, drink, live, and are sometimes conceived in these four-wheeled friends. The state-of-the-art in transportation is displayed at the **Transcenter**, and some of the futuristic-looking vehicles are actually available today.

Between the World of Motion and **Journey Into Imagination** is the gateway to World Showcase, which is described later. Continuing with Future World, it is worth noting that Walt Disney always stressed the importance of imagination, and Journey Into Imagination exhorts Disney's guests to exercise their own.

The last two themed areas are **The Land**, and **The Living Seas**. The first uses Audio-Animatronics to good effect, where the Kitchen Krackpots provide a musical send-up of our daily foods. One can also cruise through a food technology review and examine the dependence humanity has on the land. The Living Seas looks at that other important source of food, and boasts the largest man-made 'ocean' in the world. At Sea Base Alpha their 5.7-million gallon underwater environment surrounds the visitor in a world filled with the bright flash of tropical fish, sharks, dolphins, and the endangered manatee. Marine scientists are on hand to answer questions about the most spectacular man-made coral reef ever, and the frequent dives into the tank are narrated and educational. The Coral Reef Restaurant is very popular and diners should book early.

In the 'other half' of EPCOT Center **World Showcase** propels the visitor through eleven (soon to be thirteen) countries. Of course it is impossible to fully represent a massive, multifaceted country like China, and yet the spectacle they have achieved literally leaves the audience reeling. And the showcase is a great place to buy quality souvenirs from around the world. Each country has 'pop-up' entertainment, and at varying times during the day one may see traditional song, dance, or mime. The countries are wrapped around one of Walt Disney World's many lakes, which is crisscrossed by boats. At night the lake reflects the colourful 'IllumiNations'.

Disney have solved the dilemma faced by jet-set tourists — purchases are whisked through hyperspace to the Package Pickup Point, where they may be collected when leaving EPCOT Center.

Clockwise from the World Showcase entrance is **Mexico** where the visitor may cruise through the Aztec-inspired architecture and the River of Time. The great civilizations of Mexico are remembered there, and also in an exhibition entitled the Art of Mexico. Both the San Angel Inn Restaurant and the more informal Cantina de San Angel offer Mexican food and drink. Next door to Mexico is **Norway**. Here the Maelstrom is a fun cruise through Norwegian legend, where those braving the perils of sea and trolls are rewarded with the undisputed beauty of Norway.

The Temple of Heaven is the epitome of architecture in **China**, a serene reflection when viewed through the Lotus Pond. The Yong Feng Shangdian (Bountiful Harvest) gift shop is well named. It has an incredible selection of 'souvenirs', from a pair of bamboo chop-

*Disney-MGM make stunts look simple*  (© The Walt Disney Company)

sticks to massive jade ornaments. Chinese embroidery, art, decorative vases large enough to grow trees in, and china are all there, ready to be boxed and shipped home. The 360 degree panorama at the Wonders of China presentation is the next best thing to a trip down the Yangtze, but remember to hold onto the handrails.

**Germany** has no rides or movies, not that those enjoying the year-round *Oktoberfest* mind. The shops are well stocked, whether one is looking for a teddy bear, a beer *stein*, or a selection of their delectable cookies and chocolate. In **Italy** it's the L'Originale Alfredo di Roma Ristorante, which, like the German Biergarten, should be booked in advance. However, the good old fashioned hot dogs, hamburgers, and mom's apple pie of **America** require no reservation. The main attraction is the American Adventure, where an Audio-Animatronics Ben Franklin and Mark Twain play host to a multimedia review of America and its people.

To enjoy or to become acquainted with Japanese cuisine, where better than **Japan**. A reservation is recommended in the Teppanyaki Dining Rooms, but two other restaurants respectively offer *sushi* and *tempura*. Traditional and contemporary art may be found in Japan, as can the very well stocked Mitsukoshi Department Store. At **Morocco** the country's art, history, and architecture are on exhibit, but uncharacteristically the traders are not keen to bargain.

**France** is next, with the Impressions de France, a cinematic montage of classical music and scenes of the French countryside. The restaurants are particularly popular and usually require a reservation. Early visitors might care to sample a fresh *croissant* or two.

Beyond is the International Gateway, where holders of 4 and 5 day tickets and resort residents may make connections with other parts of the Walt Disney World Resort. Then it is off to the **United Kingdom**, where one may partake of afternoon tea or down a pint of best beer and play darts at the Rose & Crown Pub. Gifts are available from throughout the UK, and Disney must be congratulated for reminding Americans that there is such a place as Wales.

A resounding chorus of the national anthem of **Canada** completes this circumnavigation of World Showcase, and once more the screen is a panoramic 360 degrees. This spectacular tribute is guaranteed to make everyone yearn for the natural beauty of Canada.

EPCOT Center does not close before 9pm, with extended hours in summer and during peak holidays. Every evening the World Showcase explodes into the 'IllumiNations'. Lasers and fireworks light up the night sky in a spectacular send off, but do not forget to stop at the Package Pickup Point on the way out for your purchases.

# Disney-MGM Studios Theme Park

The third and latest Walt Disney World extravaganza, is the Disney-   ✳
MGM Studios Theme Park. Where else could Indiana Jones rub
shoulders with Miss Piggy, or Roger Rabbit exchange tips with
Mickey Mouse? The Disney-MGM Studios Theme Park combines
some of the best moments of motion pictures and television with the
latest in special effects. Behind the scenes tours show how the movies
were made, and at the backstage tour of the live, working studios, the
future is revealed. Yet to be seen episodes of television programmes,
scenes from the next big-screen blockbuster, anything could be
happening. Even if all shooting is at a hiatus, which it can be, Disney
Company still have a trick or two up their sleeve.

The usual recommendations about not losing your car and arriving early to purchase tickets apply. Prospective visitors *may* see more
in the actual working studios on weekdays — but there is always
plenty to see and do. The Production Information Window at the
main entrance answers questions on production activities, shooting
schedules, and studio audience ticket availability. Audience participation is a major part of a day at Disney-MGM Studios, adding to
the fun and early arrivals can volunteer for all sorts of predicaments.

Beyond the main entrance the visitor steps onto **Hollywood
Boulevard**. Collectors of Hollywood memorabilia would kill for the
props or one-time possessions of the stars at Sid Cahuenga's One-of-
a-Kind. Budding stars can make their own videos at Calling Dick
Tracy or Sights & Sounds, but be early to avoid the crush.

While heading for the main attractions, look for THE SIGN OF THE
TIMES. It lists the busy schedule of the day's events. Many of the tours
roll continuously, and likely waiting times are listed. Times of
important events, such as the Indiana Jones Stunt Spectacular, can be
written on the Theme Park Map. Keep an eye out for famous stars, at
least one appears daily, and also for larger-than-life versions of the
*Muppets*, Disney characters like *Pluto*, *Goofy*, and *Donald*, plus *Roger
Rabbit*, *Dick Tracy*, and *Teenage Mutant Ninja Turtles*.

The **Disney-MGM Studios Animation Tour** comes last in the
Disney handout guide, but visitors may wish to go there first
(everyone else goes straight for the Backstage Studio Tour or The
Great Movie Ride). The Animation Tour encompasses all the Disney
Magic, starting with a trip Back to Never Land. This is simultaneously amusing and enlightening, as the stages of creating a cartoon
unfold. The audience is then led through a real animation studio,
where each element of production is displayed on screen above a
room where the actual work takes place. After each of the ten stages
have been demonstrated in turn, all the magical moments of Disney

animation are relived in the Disney Classics Theater.

The **Chinese Theatre**, back along Hollywood Boulevard, is where guests take *The Great Movie Ride*, a romp through movies past, present, and future. Of course Hollywood Boulevard wouldn't be what it is without the stars, and many have come to Disney-MGM Studio. The nearby Theatre of the Stars has a song and dance tribute to cinema starring the characters created by Disney.

At **SuperStar Television** members of the audience are the real stars. Volunteers are cast to appear on major television programmes. Budding news readers, soap opera heros and pop stars should make their way forward. The latest high-tech editing puts them on screen with their favourite stars. The theme of participation is also strong at the **Monster Sound Show**, where a haunted house becomes peopled with ghosts and ghouls that shriek in the night. Noise-making skills may be further honed at the SoundWorks and Soundsations.

There are age and health restrictions at **Star Tours**, a thrill ride created by George Lucas and Disney. The show actually begins in the queue, so even those who cannot ride may tag along for the first half. Cute little robots scurry around the Star Base repair facility.

Do not miss the **Indiana Jones Epic Stunt Spectacular**. The entrances are roped off before the excitement begins, and there are only a limited number of shows. Given the nature of the production — all the best stunts from *Raiders of the Lost Ark* performed live — Disney cannot be blamed for not wanting distractions. Members of the audience are once again called to volunteer, but do not worry, they rarely get caught in the explosive finale.

The **Backstage Studio Tour** comes in two parts, both of which are usually less crowded in the afternoon. The **Shuttle Tour** embarks on a half-hour ride past the costumes, scenery, props, and sets which create almost any desired cinematic atmosphere. At Catastrophe Canyon a disaster scene from cinema history is recreated by modern technology. Passengers seated on the left of the trolley get wet.

The shuttle ride ends at New York, which has been recreated for filming at Disney-MGM, and where many of the movie characters pop up along the backlot streets. Signs in the backlot plaza point to both toilets and the hour long **Walking Tour** which takes you through the backstage production areas, starting with the Water Effects Tank. That and the Special Effects Workshop are firm favourites, and the latter includes techniques used in the latest Disney films. Photography and videoing of any kind is not allowed in the Soundstages, where television episodes and scenes from movies may be filming. Although nothing is guaranteed to be happening on any given day, even when the sets are on hiatus or behind screens of

*Close encounters with
Shamu the killer whale
at Sea World*

*Hanna-Barbera
cartoons come to life at
Universal Studios*

secrecy, Disney-MGM give an excellent tour.

*Here Come the Muppets*, an off-Broadway live musical starring Kermit and company is onthe newer productions. Additions and enhancements are planned throughout the Disney-MGM Studios Theme Park and the rest of Walt Disney World. Nothing is static, and the Disney motto is, 'Everything is subject to change'.

# Sea World

Shamu and crew welcome visitors to Sea World of Florida with a flourish and a splash. Sea World can be found off Interstate 4, halfway between Orlando and Walt Disney World, and they are owned and operated by Busch Entertainment Corporation, who also run Busch Gardens and Cypress Gardens. The Florida chapter of Sea World has been around since 1973, and they remain one of Florida's top entertainment centres.

Sea World has a number of thrilling shows and informative exhibits, and a day there can involve considerable dashing back and forth. The exhibits are open from 9am onwards, and daytime shows usually run at least twice, so the visitor may prefer to see the exhibits first, before they tire, then sit through the later series of shows.

Sea World has two optional extra guided tours. At Behind-the-Scenes visitors learn about park operation, and the vital role Sea World expertise plays in rescuing and rehabilitating stranded marine mammals. Lets Talk Training includes an actual training session, highlighting the bond between trainer and animal. Both tours can fill up, so interested parties should book at the ticket booth or at the information counter immediately beyond the main entrance.

There are numerous chances to touch or feed the inhabitants. Dolphin petting at the Dolphin Community Pool is better first thing, when the chances are good that one will come within easy reach. Once the nearby fish stall opens they check hands moving towards them for fish, and can be very fickle when it runs out. Visitors can also feed the animals at the Seal Lion and Seal Community Pool. Between the dolphin and sea lion pools is the 160,000 gallon Tropical Reef.

Sea World's stingray lagoon is safe, as are the starfish and sea urchin encounters at the Tide Pool, while visitors are shielded from the antarctic air-conditioning of the Penguin Encounter. The freezing climate is enjoyed by the penguins and the state-of-the-art habitat gives visitors a bird's-eye view above and below water. Check the park map and show schedules for penguin feeding time.

At Sharks! the peoplemover takes guests right through the midst of the most efficient predators in the world. Two presentations highlight sharks and their role in the marine environment, while petite sharks inhabit the smaller tanks, where they are more visible. Other displays and things to see include Sand Sculpture, the Pelican Exhibit, the Sky Tower, and Cap'n Kid's World.

The Whale and Dolphin Discovery Show provides a great intro-duction to the world of marine mammals, specifically the Atlantic bottlenose dolphins, beluga whales, and the false killer whales. Over at the Sea Lion & Otter Stadium, Clyde and Seamore offer a little light relief, with the help of a friendly otter and a wacky walrus.

The Sea World Ski Team puts on action-packed performances in front of the Atlantis Water Ski Stadium, while across the lake is the Nautilus Showplace, which specializes in acrobatic acts. Over at the Polynesian Revue in the South Seas Beach Stage is a preview of the Sea World Polynesian Luau held each evening (reservations rec-ommended for this extra).

James Earl Jones narrates the introduction to *Shamu: New Visions*, where a 15ft by 20ft video screen brings visitors closer than ever to the excitement. The action takes place in the 5-million gallon habitat that Shamu and the other killer whales call home, with excellent views from the stadium seating. By using cameras above and below the surface mixed with a judicious amount of background footage, the audience is right there with trainers and killer whales.

Sea World of Florida provide all the amenities necessary for a complete vacation experience: gift shops, restaurants, snack bars, seal lion and dolphin food, first aid, stroller and wheelchair rental, pet shelters, and foreign currency exchange. Currently they are the only major theme park outside Spaceport USA that does not charge for parking. With plenty of opportunity to sit and watch the shows, plus the lack of long queues (there are no rides), Sea World is a most enjoyable Orlando theme park. Before leaving give the park map and show schedule another quick glimpse — the daytime shows are replaced by new ones at night, including a laser and fireworks spectacular during the peak summer season and selected holidays.

# Universal Studios                                              ✳

Outside Hollywood, there is no film and television studio larger than Universal Studios Florida. Billboards proclaim such major motion pictures as *Ghost Busters*, *Back to the Future*, *King Kong*, and *E.T.*, but people do not go to Universal to see the films — but to star in them.

Comfortable shoes are vital as there is much to see in a day which will include long periods of standing. Services from foreign lan-guage brochures to lost children are handled by guest relations near the entrance, while banking and currency exchange is just past the gate in the Front Lot. Universal produce a guide for the handicapped, detailing rides and tours accessible to them.

The busy section straight ahead upon entering the studios is Production Central, with the *FUNtastic World of Hanna-Barbera* on the left. All the cartoon gang is there, and once guests have been briefed on the arts of cartoon making, they are sent on a mission with Yogi Bear and Boo Boo to rescue Elroy Jetson.

Behind the FUNtastic World the *Nickelodeon Studios* shows behind the scenes of a television network just for children. Young actors can request a screen test after the tour, or audience tickets for a live taping. The *Production Tour* is a less zany, gentle tour outside the main production buildings.

The next event, *Alfred Hitchcock: The Art of Making Movies*, comes with a PG13 warning. The show is in three stages, and parents can opt to skip the first two should they or their children feel squeamish. The first part involves the master himself taking his victims, the audience, through clippings of his fifty films, including the first showing of the 3-D version of *Dial M for Murder*. Survivors proceed to a re-enactment of the *Psycho* shower scene, with the murderer selected from the audience. The third section is pure participation, where 'volunteers' show how the effects were created.

The whole of Manhattan is crowded into the sets of **New York**. The dramatic rooftop scene of *Ghostbusters* is re-enacted, in front of the audience, with special effects thought possible only on film. Then, after being filmed with favourite stars in the *Screen Test Video Adventure*, it is into the heart of the New York Subway for the *Kongfrontation*. The queueing crowds attempt to escape the ape via an aerial tram, only to find themselves falling into his clutches.

**San Fransisco** is the scene for *Earthquake, The Big One*. In the evening there's more mayhem with *Dynamite Nights Stunt Spectacular*, a thrill-packed set of stunts performed live on the lagoon, involving government agents, drug dealers, and some fancy boating. Meanwhile, **Expo Center** has some of the latest additions to Universal Studios. For a blast to the past, nothing can beat *Back to the Future: The Ride*. Guests learn all the secrets in Doc Brown's top-security laboratory, including his latest eight seat time-traveller. The thrill-packed trip is great fun, but health and age restrictions apply.

For a more relaxed pace, the nearby *E.T. Adventure* is much slower, including the queues. After saving E.T.'s planet, guests can wander over to the World's Largest *Hard Rock Café*, full of music, memorabilia, and pure American food. The café is open until late, and can be accessed from inside or outside the studios. Meanwhile, at the *Animal Actors Stage*, Lassie, Benji, Mr Ed, and a whole cast of four-footed stars put on a great act.

Schwab's Pharmacy is *the* place to be discovered in **Hollywood**, but do not eat there before visiting the *Phantom of the Opera Make Up Show*. The gruesome secrets of the horror movies are revealed in technicolour detail, from amazing transformations to recipes for realistic gore. It is rated PG13 — children, hold your parents' hands.

# Kissimmee

The road between Walt Disney World and Kissimmee, US Highway 192, is littered with motels, fast food, crazy golf, restaurants, and amusements of all descriptions, with themes from the Middle Ages to a house of the future. Driving is more relaxed south from Kissimmee, through the orange and cattle country. Although quieter than the tourist triangle, there's plenty to see and do, but first, we will look at selected attractions along US Highway 192.

There are (at last count) four **Dinner Extravaganzas** in Kissimmee,  all on Highway 192. The closest to Disney is *Arabian Nights Dinner*, where a princess searches for her beloved prince, with the help of a genie and a cast of dozens of horses. Royal Lipizzans and Arabian horses are only part of the entertainment, while the meal is prime rib plus accoutrements. Evening guests at the *Fort Liberty Dinner Show & Trading Post* are treated to fine food and entertainment. Meals are also served in the daytime, when the fort, western village, gift shops and waxworks become a mini theme park. The evenings at the *Medieval Times and Life* are full of the clash of swords, pikes, and shields, as the knights show their skills in displays and tournaments. By day it is a complete village straight from the Middle Ages, with thatched roofs, cobblestone streets and period artisans. Although not a dinner extravaganza as such, *Little Darlin's Rock 'N' Roll Palace* at Old Town Kissimmee does offer entertainment straight from the '50s, with bars and a dining facility. Guests can dance or watch others swing to top entertainers from the '50s and '60s. Also in the Old Town shopping and entertainment complex is the Superstars Hall of Fame, with memorabilia from Elvis Presley, Marilyn Monroe, the Beatles and many others.

Between the dinner shows, hotels, go carts, airboat rides, and crazy golf courses is Water Mania. There are water slides, a wave pool, oceanless beaches and picnic facilities. At nearby Xanadu, the  home of the future combines energy efficiency with computerized environmental control and entertainment.

Also in the Kissimmee area is the **Flying Tigers Warbird Air**  **Museum**, located off Highway 192 on Hoagland Boulevard (Airport Road). Here are preserved vintage airplanes, and in addition to the static display one may see World War II and other aircraft being restored to flying condition. Lucky visitors may see a test flight.

Back on Highway 192 is Alligatorland Safari Zoo, one of Florida's innumerable alligator-themed attractions. Cold blooded creatures may also to be seen at Reptile World Serpentarium on 192, while Gatorland Zoo is between Kissimmee and Orlando. Also along Highway 17/92 is the free Tupperware Dish Museum, with a guided factory tour and a museum of containers through the ages.

## Cattle and Orange Country

Kissimmee has shaken off its dusty cow town image, but to the south the busy tourist triangle changes to a countryside dotted with cattle and orange groves. At Haines City, Highway 17/92 joins Highway 27, which has all the amenities a traveller could want. Alternate 27, the old road just east of the main 27, has less traffic and stop lights, and more scenery. Davidson of Dundee on the new Highway 27 has a citrus candy factory, where you can taste before buying. At Dundee drivers must decide whether to continue on Highway 27 or detour west to Cypress Gardens.

To the south of Dundee at **Lake Wales**, agriculture is the town's primary source of income, although tourism is growing. **Bok Tower Gardens** is the most prominent attraction, located on the highest point of land in southern Florida. Edward Bok had the hill transformed into a landscaped garden and, remembering his childhood in Norway, he added a marble and coquina carillon tower (not open to the public). The bells should be heard from a slight distance. Short selections are played throughout the day, with a full recital every day at 3pm. The visitor centre is in an old cracker house, and other facilities include a garden café, gift shop, picnic area, free wheelchairs and pushchairs, and a self-guided tour of the extensive gardens.

Within Lake Wales is **The Depot**, a onetime railway depot which is now a free museum and cultural centre. There are displays to interest history and railway buffs, and numerous changing handicraft exhibits. In late winter and early spring to the south of Lake Wales is the Black Hills Passion Play. This sensitive production has won considerable acclaim in the more than fifty years it has been performed in South Dakota, and Lake Wales has been its winter home for almost that long. Schedules alter each year, with extra performances on Good Friday and Easter Sunday.

Just west of Lake Wales on Florida 60 is **Lake Kissimmee State Park**, right in the heart of cattle country. On weekends the state park's living history programme proudly presents the Kissimmee Cow Catcher. The year is 1876, and the catcher is getting ready to drive another herd of cattle down the cracker trail to Punta Rassa (near Fort Myers). The long-horned cattle found in the pens today are descendants of those the Spanish brought from Andalusia and released hundreds of years ago.

The Cow Camp is only a small part of this massive park, which has something for everyone. Nature trails vary from a short walk to back country hikes to primitive campsites. Rental boats and canoes are available as well as food, soft drinks, and fishing accessories. The pontoon boats are great for fishing or a family picnic/party on the lake, while canoeists can spend all day exploring the canals and waterways. The 5 mile (8km) round trip trail from the park entrance to the main campground is littered with deer and other wildlife, especially early and late in the day. Bird spotting is excellent. The park is especially blessed with bald eagles and the Everglades snail kite, which is elusive elsewhere.

The grand old belle of Winter Haven (and Florida) is **Cypress Gardens**, which first opened its gates 1936. The late Dick Pope saw his garden grow fourteen-fold from its original beginnings with sixteen acres. Over the years the character of the gardens developed, with both water-ski shows and southern belles. Today some forty gardeners maintain the accredited botanical gardens, which are in bloom 365 days of the year. A bevy of belles circle the gardens, dressed in antebellum fashion.

If a stroll through the gardens of a now-vanished South does not appeal, the other side of the park will. Turn left at the entrance for a totally different Cypress Gardens. The star attraction is the water-ski show, which involves a number of ski boats and expert skiers. The well produced and executed show combines comedy, trick skiing, and a dozen set pieces that would be the grand finale elsewhere. The new Kodak Island in the Sky is a massive carousel which rotates slowly (for photography), over 150ft above the gardens. Two different boat rides run regularly, one into the gardens, the other around the lake. Cypress Gardens is an accredited zoo, with the usual bird and reptile shows, and they exhibit the 'Nation's most elaborate model railroad'.

## Greater Orlando

With its international airport and interconnecting highways, Orlando is the gateway to central Florida. **International Drive** in southwest Orlando has good shopping, and evening entertainment in the form of dining extravaganzas. Both can be found at **Mercado Mediterranean Village**, which has a wide range of shops and restaurants in addition to the Mardi Gras Dinner and Variety Show. The

Official Orlando & Orange County **Visitor Center** is also at Mercado, and they can help choose a hotel/motel. Just down the road is King Henry's Feast, another dinner spectacle, with a medieval flavour.

The area surrounding International Drive has theme and amusement parks such as Sea World and Universal Studios. Near the latter is the Mystery Fun House, a cross between an old-fashioned circus fun house, a miniature golf course, and the inside of an arcade game. South of Universal is **Wet 'N Wild** with the Black Hole, Hydra Maniac, Knee Ski, and Blue Niagara for the thrill seekers; a new section specifically for youngsters; and the lazy river for relaxing. Nearby is the Elvis Presley Museum, exhibiting some of the best of the King's memorabilia, straight from Graceland.

More shopping can be found on International Drive at **Belz Factory Outlet World**, with 160 or so manufacturers selling their wares direct. **Florida Mall** on Sand Lake Road has four main department stores, plenty of fashion, clothing, and accessories boutiques, plus restaurants and services, such as an air ticketing agency. Those who love shopping or who find the location convenient (midway between the Airport and International Drive), can stay at the Sheraton Plaza Hotel.

**Church Street Station**, off Interstate 4 Junction 28, is downtown Orlando's premier entertainment, shopping, and dining complex. The Exchange has some sixty specialty shops and eateries, plus Commander Ragtime's video games and circus memorabilia. In the evening a cover charge applies, but shopping and the Commander's is always free admission. The original Rosie O'Grady's nightspot has a Dixieland Jazz atmosphere, and the four other showplaces offer bluegrass and folk, top forty hits, country and western, and live music from the '50s to the '70s. Between 11am and 2am there is always something going on at Church Street Station, with free entertainment during the daytime. The dining varies from bar snacks to fine cuisine, and there are often specials during weekdays. It is worth asking Church Street Station ahead of time for bus transport, if your hotel does not provide it.

Given the strip development surrounding Orlando, one might expect the downtown area to be the same. Iinstead it is a city of tall buildings, clean streets, and plenty of parks. Lake Eola Park is within strolling distance of Church Street Station, and has shade trees and a central fountain. **Loch Haven Park** is a short drive north, signposted from Interstate 4. Within the large park is the Orange County Historical Museum, with exhibits from Orlando's younger days and a restored fire station. Also in the park are the Science Center, Museum of Art, and the Civic Theater of Central Florida. At

*Holidaymakers know when they are in Orlando*

*Church Street Station is a smorgasbord of dining and entertainment*

least a day could be spend browsing through the park's offerings: displays of pre-Columbian and American Art, the Seminole War and the orange industry's booms and busts, a planetarium show, and a mystery or comedy.

The dogwood, azaleas and camellias of **Leu Botanical Gardens** harken back to the early 1900s, which were boom years for farming in Orange County, with tours of the rather luxurious farmhouse included. The nearby Mead Botanical Gardens are more a public picnic and recreation area than a formal garden.

Upmarket shopping can be found along the tree-lined Park Avenue of Winter Park, which is a great area to park and stroll. East from Park Avenue on Welbourne is the **Morse Gallery of Art**. Many pieces on display are the works of Louis Comfort Tiffany, which were rescued from the ashes of Laurelton Hall, his home on Long Island. The Morse Gallery is renowned for its fine collection of Art Nouveau.

Beyond the urban sprawl of Orlando and environs is the old Florida, rapidly being engulfed by the suburbs of the suburbs. **Wekiwa Springs State Park**, a short excursion to the north, offers a break from the pressures of busy Orlando. The refreshing waters of the spring can be swum year-round, or you can explore the local waterways with a rental canoe. Overnight canoeists can get kitted out at Katie's Wekiwa River Landing. Relaxing land-based activities include picnicking and short walks, with 15 miles (24km) of trails available for longer jaunts. The campsites are surrounded by trees, but have modern amenities, such as water and electric hookups and hot showers. The spring is, of course, nature's own jacuzzi.

The northeast corner of Central Florida is **Sanford**, head of navigation of the St Johns River. Nearby are two parks, The Senator with a 3,500-year-old giant cypress tree, and the Central Florida Zoological Park. However, most people visit Sanford for a river cruise, and amongst the ships departing regularly are the riverboat *Princess* and the rivership *Grand Romance*. The latter has a luncheon and evening cruise on the St Johns River in their 'wedding cake' showboat, complete with food, drink and entertainment.

# Additional Information

## Visitor Information

Kissimmee/St Cloud Convention
& Visitors Bureau
1925 E Irlo Bronson Memorial Hwy
Kissimmee FL 34744
☎ 407-847-5000 or 800-327-9159

Lake County Tourist Development
Council
315 West Main St
Tavares FL 32778
☎ 904-343-9850

Polk County Tourist Development
Council
600 N Broadway, Suite 300
Bartow FL 33830
☎ 813-534-6066

Orlando/Orange County
Convention & Visitors Bureau
7208 Sand Lake Road
Orlando FL 32819
☎ 407-363-5800

## Local Events

*Feb to Easter*
Black Hills Passion Play
Alt US 27, Lake Wales
Performance times vary

*Early Feb*
Florida Citrus Festival
Winter Haven

*Mid-late Feb*
Kissimmee Valley Livestock Show
& County Fair
Next to Rodeo Grounds,
Kissimmee

*Mid-late Feb and late June*
Silver Spurs Rodeo
Silver spurs arena, Kissimmee

*Late Feb, early March*
Florida Strawberry Festival
Plant City

*Early March*
Kissimmee Bluegrass Festival
(Country & Gospel Music)
Silver Spurs Arena, Kissimmee

*End Oct, early Nov*
Florida State Air Fair
Kissimmee Airport

*End Dec*
Warbird Weekend
Flying Tigers Warbird Air Museum
Kissimmee

## Places of Interest

### Apopka
*Wekiwa Springs State Park*
1800 Wekiwa Circle
FL 32712
☎ 407-889-9920
Open: 8am-sunset
Swimming, canoe rental, snacks,
picnic, camp, hike, ♿

### Kissimmee
*Flying Tigers Warbird Air Museum*
231 N Airport Road
FL 34741
☎ 407-933-1942
Open: 9am-6.30pm, 9am-8pm summer
Guided tours

*Old Town Kissimmee*
5770 W Irlo Bronson Memorial Hwy
FL 34746
☎ 407-396-4888
Open: 10am-10pm, free
Shopping, dining, rides, entertainment, ♿

*Water Mania*
6073 West Irlo Bronson Hwy
(US 192)
FL 34746
☎ 407-396-2626
Open: 10am-5pm spring and
autumn, 9am-9pm summer, closed
winter
Water amusements, picnic, ♿

*Xanadu, Home of the Future*
4800 W Irlo Bronson Memorial Hwy
(Space Coast Highway)
FL 32741
☎ 407-396-1922
Open: 10am-late
Computerized hi-tech home, tours

**Lake Wales**
*Bok Tower Gardens*
PO Drawer 3810 (Off US 27)
FL 33853
☎ 813-676-1408
Open: 8am-5pm and selected evenings
Carillon recitals, tower, gardens,
restaurant, picnic, gifts

*Lake Kissimmee State Park*
14248 Camp Mack Rd
(East on Route 60)
FL 33853
☎ 813-696-1112
Open: 8am-sunset
Weekend Cow Camp, boat & canoe
rental, picnic, hike, camp, &

**Orlando**
*The Depot*
101 South Boyd St
Winter Garden FL 34787
☎ 407-656-8749
Open: 9am-5pm Mon-Fri, 10am-
4pm Sat, except holidays, free
Railway cars, model railway
exhibit, crafts, gifts

*Elvis Presley Museum*
6544 Carrier Drive
FL 32819
☎ 407-345-9427
Hours vary
Tours, gifts

*Gatorland Zoo*
14501 South Orange Blossom Trail
FL 32821
☎ 407-855-5496
Open: 9am-6pm, extended in
summer
Alligators, mini-zoo, gifts, snacks,
&

*Leu Botanical Gardens*
1730 North Forest Ave
FL 32803
☎ 407-849-2620
Open: 9am-5pm except Xmas
Gardens, farmhouse museum

*Mercado Mediterranean Village*
8445 International Drive
FL 32819
☎ 407-345-9337
Open: 10am-10pm, free
Shopping, information centre,
restaurants, entertainment, &

*Morse Museum of American Art*
133 East Wellbourne Ave
Winter Park FL 32789
☎ 407-644-3686
Open: 9.30am-4pm Tue-Sat except
holidays. Tours

*Mystery Fun House*
5767 Major Blvd
FL 32819
☎ 407-351-3356
Open: 10am-9pm, 10am-10pm in
spring and summer. Mini-golf,
arcades, rides, gifts, restaurant

*Orlando Museum of Art*
2416 North Mills Ave
FL 32803
☎ 407-896-4231
Hours vary, closed Mon
Gifts, tours, &

*Sea World of Florida*
7007 Sea World Drive
FL 32821
☎ 305-351-3600
(01-637-7961 from UK)
Open: 9am daily, closing varies
Numerous shows & exhibits,
restaurants, gifts, tours, &

*Universal Studios Florida*
1000 Universal Studios Plaza
FL 32819-7610
☎ 407-363-8000
Open: 9am, closing varies seasonally
Working studios, rides, restaurants, gifts, Hard Rock Cafe, &

*Walt Disney World Resort*
PO Box 10,040
(Off I-4 south of Orlando)
Lake Buena Vista FL 32830-0040
☎ 407-824-4321
Theme parks open at 9am, closing
varies
Magic Kingdom, Epcot Center,
Disney-MGM Studios, Resorts,
Disney Village, &

*Wet'n Wild*
6200 International Drive
FL 32819
☎ 407-351-1800
Open: varies, closed winter
Innumerable water rides, food,
gifts, children's section

## Winter Haven
*Cypress Gardens*
PO Box 1 (West of US 27)
Cypress Gardens FL 33884
☎ 813-324-2111 or 800-237-4826
Open: 9am-6pm with extensions
Water ski show, gardens, restau-
rant & snacks, boat rides, &

## Evening Dinner/ Entertainment

## Kissimmee
*Arabian Nights Dinner*
6225 W Irlo Bronson Memorial
    Hwy
FL 32746
☎ 407-239-9223 or 800-553-6116
Open evenings
&

*Fort Liberty Wild West Dinner Show
    & Trading Post*
5260 US 192
FL 34741
☎ 407-351-5151 or 800-347-8181
Open: 7.30am, dinner 6.30pm and
9pm, shows vary
Fort, entertainment, restaurant,
gifts

*Little Darlin's Rock 'N' Roll Palace*
5770 W Irlo Bronson Memorial Hwy
FL 34741
☎ 407-396-6499
Evenings
Entertainment, bars, dining

*Medieval Life & Times*
PO Box 2385 (4510 Highway 192)
FL 32742
☎ 407-239-0214, 407-396-1518
or 800-432-0768
Open: 9am-9pm
Medieval village, evening dinner &
show, gifts, &

## Orlando
*Church Street Station*
129 West Church St
FL 32801
☎407-442-2434
Open: 11am-2am daily
Evening cover charge
Entertainment, bars, restaurants,
snacks, shopping, &

*King Henry's Feast*
8984 International Drive
FL 32819
☎ 407-351-5151 or 800-347-8181
Open evenings
Banquet, entertainment, drinks
included

*Mardi Gras at
Mercado Mediterranean Village*
8445 International Drive
FL 32819
☎ 407-351-5151 or 800-347-8181
Open evening
Jazz band, meal & drinks included,
&

## Tours and Transportation

## Sanford
*Riverboat Grand Romance*
443 N Palmetto Ave
FL 32771
☎ 407-321-5091
Scenic and dining cruises

# 6

# *THE GOLD COAST*

---

Wealth comes in many guises, and the Gold Coast is blessed with most of them. Fort Lauderdale, Palm Beach, and Jupiter Island are havens for the rich. Sunken Spanish Galleons have left a rich heritage along the Gold Coast, and rumours suggest still more is buried inland. The golden sunshine and glittering sands bring others who, for a time, live like royalty in Flagler-era resorts. But a vast fortune is not necessary to experience the grandeur of Henry Flagler's mansion home, or to sample the riches of the Gold Coast.

## Greater Fort Lauderdale

Even in its earliest days, Fort Lauderdale had profound effects upon its visitors. There were three successive forts which the town was named after, and frontier soldiers there went on to become great generals during the Civil War. In later years hoards of students turned Fort Lauderdale upside-down during Spring College Break. Today the Seminole Indians are friendly and the students prefer Daytona Beach, so it is perfectly safe for visitors to find the effect Fort Lauderdale has on them.

Fort Lauderdale is a residential resort, with hundreds of miles of canals and waterways, most of them navigable, prompting it's claim to be the largest yacht basin in America. The wealth is conspicuous and ubiquitous, with a refreshing absence of snobbery. The owner of a custom-designed yacht will happily wave and chat to a weekend visitor in a rubber dinghy. Those without a boat can always catch a water taxi or make waves on a tour of the canals.

Fort Lauderdale is synonymous with beaches, and public access is excellent. Meter parking is available along the three-mile stretch of Atlantic Boulevard, with some free parking on the northern section,  across from the **Hugh Taylor Birch State Recreation Area**. Given the hot sub-tropical sun, it may be better to park here as the trees provide shade and a tunnel gives beach access. Acclimatization is easier if the hottest part of the day is spent picnicking or enjoying a bite to eat at the park concession, or exploring the historic home owned by Hugh Taylor Birch, who donated the property to the state.

For those with an inclination towards the nautical, long term parking is also available at the Bahia Mar Marina and Resort. Numerous charter boats, sailboats, dive boats to local reefs, and the *Jungle Queen* depart from Bahia Mar. The latter is one of Fort  Lauderdale's oldest traditions, but operating with large new 'paddlewheelers'. Their mini-cruise takes in the multimillion dollar homes along the waterways. Daytime is best for seeing the gardens and gardeners, while at night the residents come alive. Strangely enough, the wealthy people waving their arms from the comfort of their homes are not shaking their fists. Despite the massive search-light used by the *Jungle Queen* to illuminate the properties, everyone is friendly, and often pause in mid-barbeque to wave a thick steak or marinated drumstick. The evening cruise includes a meal with 'all you wish to eat', a vaudeville act, and a sing-a-long back to Bahia Mar. Landlubbers can see Fort Lauderdale from the Voyager Sightseeing Train, which departs from nearby.

Just up from Bahia Mar on Seabreeze Avenue is the **International**  **Swimming Hall of Fame**. Recognizable from its wave-shaped building, it has numerous hands-on exhibits, several pools where competitions are held and top athletes train, and displays highlighting great swimmers of the world. The Hall of Fame collects memorabilia and gives detailed histories of those who have contributed significantly to swimming and diving.

Shopping in Fort Lauderdale is a matter of taste and budget. The **Galleria**, inland from Hugh Taylor Birch SRA on Sunrise Boulevard, hosts numerous shops and restaurants, plus notable department stores. Further out on Sunrise, north of the junction with Flamingo Road, is the more budget conscious Sawgrass Mills, where visitors should wear comfortable shoes to walk its mile-long corridor.

The main road from downtown Fort Lauderdale to the beach is **Las Olas Boulevard**, known for its fine shopping. The New River flows just south of Las Olas, and a great vantage point can be found by taking 6th Ave south a block and parking at the **Stranahan House**.  The house itself is the oldest remaining structure in Fort Lauderdale, and is an important link to the town's transition from frontier trading post to renowned resort. The guided tour includes the history of the area, the house and the boom and bust of owner Frank Stranahan.

In downtown Fort Lauderdale is the new **Performing Arts Center**.  The **Discovery Center**'s new Museum of Science and Discovery is scheduled for completion in late 1992. The Discovery Center will remain in the New River Inn, to be found at the historic section of Fort Lauderdale on SW 1st Avenue, until completion of the new museum. Here are numerous opportunities to learn about science and nature with excellent hands-on exhibits. The new museum will contain this, plus a multi-storey IMAX theater.

 The **Fort Lauderdale Historical Museum** is a few doors down from the New River Inn. Included are exhibits on the Seminole War, plus interesting glimpses of Fort Lauderdale's first settlers. On Saturdays at 10am the society provides a historical tour, in conjunction with the water taxi. From the Stranahan House to the Performing Arts Center is a pleasant walk alongside the New River, with the historical area and a riverside restaurant or two between.

 The downtown **Museum of Art** is popular, with frequent changes of exhibits, but their biggest attendance boost was *Flea Market Vendor* by local artist Duane Hanson. He specializes in using modern materials to create truer than life people, and most of his works are frighteningly realistic. A security guard called for paramedic assistance when Duane's sculpture failed to leave the museum in response to repeated tapping on the window. To the museum's delight, if not the guard's, the story was picked up by the national news media. Visitors

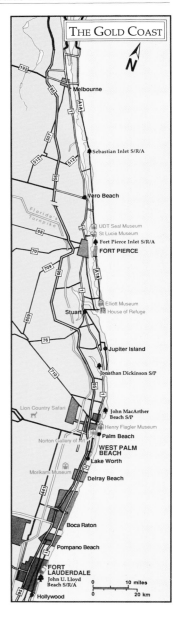

THE GOLD COAST

*Visiting the Stranahan House at Fort Lauderdale by water taxi*

*The world's largest kaleidoscope at the Discovery Centre, Fort Lauderdale*

should look for a personable lady reading a book, but do not be surprised if she does not look up.

Central Fort Lauderdale is the scene of various food festivals and dining is an important part of the Broward County/Fort Lauderdale lifestyle. The county boasts more places to eat, per head, than any other in America, and many restaurants line the north-south US Highway 1 and the old US 1, Saint Andrews Avenue.

Some of the best restaurants, and the Performing Arts Center, historical area, and the Stranahan house, can be found along the waterways — all easily accessible by using the water taxis. These floating cabs ply the New River and the Intracoastal Waterway from Commercial Boulevard in the north down to Southeast 17th Street (also known as the Brooks Memorial Causeway). In addition to a fixed price one-way fare, they offer all day tickets and weekly 'frequent floater' specials. The taxis are on call from 10am until late, and the historic river tour can booked through them. One may visit **Ocean World Dolphin Show** by water taxi, or overland via Southeast 17th Street. Although smaller than their southern neighbour, Miami Seaquarium, they put on some very slick performances.

South of Fort Lauderdale is Port Everglades, the second largest cruise port in America, with regular departures to the Caribbean, and day or half day sailings by SeaEscape and Discovery Cruises.

If time does not permit a cruise, watch the comings and goings from the beaches and picnic areas of the **John U. Lloyd Beach State Recreation Area**, on the A1A south of Fort Lauderdale. Late spring is the sea turtle nesting season, with rangers sometimes leading turtle-watches, but the beach park is great year-round. The main car parks are closest to Port Everglades, and those who love a busy, happy beach congregate there. And yet the beach nearest the entrance is quieter, great for strolling or relaxed sunning. Fewer people use that section because they the beach is hidden beyond a slightly longer boardwalk. The City of Dania fishing pier and shopping complex is at the southern entrance to the recreation area, followed by the Hollywood North Beach Park. Both State and County Parks have food concessions, picnic tables, and changing facilities.

Inland from Fort Lauderdale is **Flamingo Gardens**, just south of the Sawgrass Mills Outlet Mall. A tram tour highlights native flora as well as many exotic species. In from the Hollywood coast is the **Okalee Village Seminole Indian Reservation**, a collection of shops with Indian restaurants and a village.

North up the Gold Coast on Highway A1A are lines of condominiums, with a refreshing break in the skyline at **Lauderdale-by-the-Sea**. This more traditional seaside town has a few resort hotels and plenty of smaller motels. Then the condominiums rise once more, disappearing at the residential Hillsboro Beach, where the stretches of sand become virtually inaccessible. By Deerfield Beach the driver may be desperate for a sight of sand, but the beach-front parking meters eat quarters faster than an arcade game, with traffic wardens twice as quick. Press on another mile to the Palm Beaches.

## Palm Beach County

After settlers planted some 20,000 coconuts salvaged from a Spanish brigantine, the location *had* to be called Palm Beach. Henry Morrison Flagler envisaged a resort among the swaying fronds, and there he later built his winter residence. While the railroad went southward to Key West, Flagler was satisfied to remain at Palm Beach.

When driving northward up the coast on Highway A1A, the first city within the Palm Beach County borders is **Boca Raton**. Addison Mizner, already famous in Palm Beach for his wedding-cake Spanish revival architecture, had grand designs for Boca Raton. Despite blue-chip financial backing his property scheme collapsed, but his architectural influence remains in the Boca Raton Resort and Club, originally the Cloister Inn, and the Royal Palms Plaza Towers.

Camino Real is a pleasant palm-lined introduction to Boca Raton, a left turn for northbound drivers on the A1A, where the Boca Raton Resort and Club can be found. Drivers may turn right on NE 5th Ave and right again on Palmetto Park Road for a quick glimpse of Boca Grande and its architecture before returning to the beach; or turn left onto Palmetto to delve further. The Boca Raton Museum of the Arts is here, while the **Town Center** is right on St Andrews. The name Town Center is slightly confusing, it's actually an upmarket shopping mall with six major department stores. Left at the end of St Andrews is the Royal Palm Polo Fields, with Sunday matches from December to April. The Boca Raton beaches can be found by driving due east, turning south (right) on the Dixie Highway, and then east again on Palmetto. But to save another detour inland, first consider an interesting diversion.

Across the city line at Delray Beach is **The Morikami**, named after a philanthropic member of Yamoto, an early Japanese farming community. The Morikami is a museum, park, garden, and living culture centre illustrating ancient and modern Japan. Regular workshops bring Japanese culture to the community, and their calendar is crammed with *Origami* lessons, *Bonsai* demonstrations, tea ceremony presentations, and garden tours. The Morikami is a relaxing, refreshing diversion.

Boca Raton has numerous parks; **South Beach** and **Red Reef Parks**

*The tranquil garden at the Morikami, where Japanese culture is explained*

*For many, golf is a way of life in Palm Beach County*

sit right on the beach. The entrance fees are steep for a quick peep at the sand, but better than a day spent constantly feeding coin hungry meters. Both have picnicking, and Red Reef has a 9-hole golf course. The **Gumbo Limbo Nature Center** is opposite Red Reef Park. Everything there is free, including the interpretive centre and nature walks, but park elsewhere for the beach. **Spanish River Park** is situated north on A1A, adjacent to the Intracoastal Waterway. There are picnic tables, a children's playground, a nature walk, cycle paths, an observation tower and an access tunnel to the beach.

Other beach access along A1A between Boca Raton and Palm Beach can be found at **Atlantic Dunes Park**, **Gulf Stream Park**, **Boynton Public Beach**, and parking meters along Delray Beach. Lake Worth is primarily an inland city, possessing a long strip of land on the western shores of the Intracoastal Waterway. However, Lake Avenue crosses over to a narrow section of beach, into which is shoehorned a pier, beach club, and casino.

Like Fort Lauderdale, **Palm Beach** is a wealthy residential resort community, but there the resemblance ends. Although the inhabitants of Palm Beach value tradition over innovation, they are very active and outgoing, especially during the winter social season.

*The Breakers is a Palm Beach tradition*

Come summer many return north, and the otherwise very exclusive golf clubs become open to non-members.

**The Breakers** is synonymous with Palm Beach, although Henry Flagler would not recognize the hotel as his Palm Beach Inn of 1895. The current Italian Renaissance Palace opened its doors in 1926 for a mere six million dollars, and now the resort combines the best of fifteenth-century architecture with the latest spa and business facilities. The Breakers is an essential Palm Beach experience, even for non-residents. Guests have access to two golf courses, one on the beach and the other inland at Breakers West.

 The **Henry Morrison Flagler Museum** alone makes Palm Beach a worthy detour for those staying elsewhere (take the Tri-Rail up from Miami or Fort Lauderdale, the shuttle bus stops outside the gate). Whitehall was the name chosen by Henry Flagler and his third wife, and for a time, Whitehall was an integral part of Palm Beach society. The lavish home cost 2.5 million dollars to construct, another 1.5 million for furnishings, and literally towered over Palm Beach. The fabulous winter residence became a gentlemen's club, then a hotel, and even faced demolition, but today it is a museum of a lifestyle which few could live up to. Many of the original furnishings have been donated or bought back, while outside is Henry's personal railroad car. Charitable institutions hold fund-raising concerts in the larger ballrooms, and Whitehall is once more firmly in the Palm Beach social calendar.

There are no laws preventing sightseers from touring residential Palm Beach, as long as they refrain from trespassing or peeping through hedges. Head north on Country Road, skirting around the Palm Beach Country Club, and then up Ocean Boulevard. At the end is Lake Worth Inlet, which separates Palm Beach from Singer Island. One can return via Lake Way, which runs along the Intracoastal Waterway, known locally as Lake Worth.

The free **Hibel Museum of Art** on Poincianna Plaza houses the paintings, sculptures, and limited edition porcelains of Edna Hibel. Restaurants can be found either side of the Breakers Golf Course and some, like Testa's, offer valet parking with a garage next door, so cars can be serviced while you dine.

For sheer shopping pleasure, nothing in Florida is remotely like **Worth Avenue**. The Breakers is within easy walking distance, but one is really expected to take the car, preferably an expensive one, to the valet parking. There are parking meters on the ocean end of Worth Avenue, where less fancy automobiles are parked without disgrace. Window shopping is great along Worth Avenue; prices are rarely displayed at these exclusive shops, but if one has to ask . . . .

Across the Intracoastal Waterway is **West Palm Beach**. During the Flagler era the railroads did more than bring guests to his expensive resorts. Henry promoted agriculture along his routes, making Florida the winter garden of America. West Palm Beach housed the thousands of servants and support staff required for his Palm Beach resorts. The West Palm Beach foundation of agriculture, service and transportation has made it the largest city in Palm Beach County, with numerous parks and golf courses.

Those with young children may wish to take in the South Florida Science Museum or the nearby Dreher Park Zoo. Both of these are found within Dreher Park, and designed primarily for school children. The science museum has hands-on exhibits, aquariums with touch tanks, and a planetarium. For a more natural zoological atmosphere, **Lion Country Safari** claims to have been America's first safari park. Located inland on Southern Blvd (US Highway 98), it is a drive through open plains full of exotic animals. As the birds are not captive, Florida species mix with the African and Asian wildlife. The safari is a winter sanctuary to them, and they fly north for the summer. Convertibles may not go through Lion Country, for obvious reasons, but replacement cars are available at reasonable rates.

The eclectic tastes of Ralph and Elizabeth Norton are shared with the public at **Norton Gallery of Art**. This specially-built museum displays the cream of their permanent collection. Normally the museum rotates their permanent pieces with travelling collections. A *selection* of their important pivotal works by Gauguin, Jackson Pollock, Joos Van Cleve, George Bellows, Renoir, Tang dynasty sculptors and innumerable others are always on display.

Shopping at West Palm Beach can be almost as thrilling as Worth Avenue, if not quite so expensive. Largest are the **Gardens Mall** on PGA Boulevard, and **Palm Beach Mall** on Palm Beach Lakes Boulevard. Both are massive, offering numerous speciality shops in addition to major department stores.

Restaurants throughout Palm Beach County come in a variety of cuisines, atmospheres, and budget. For once the general steak/chicken/salad types are outnumbered by those specializing in Italian, oriental, and seafood. For a change try Greek, German, Mexican, or Cuban. Hundreds are listed in the yellow pages and the *Palm Beach County Visitor's Information Directory*.

The Port of Palm Beach is slightly north at Riviera Beach., with two- or five-day cruises on the Crown Cruise Line. The *Empress Showboat* and *Empress of Palm Beach* are sightseeing riverboats that ply the Intracoastal Waterway from **Singer Island**. Also known as Palm Beach Shores or the beach in Riviera Beach, Singer Island is a

popular resort and condominium community. Immediately north is
**John D. MacArthur Beach State Park**, with a natural beachside
setting. Singer Island holidaymakers are near enough to Palm Beach
and MacArthur State Park to have the best of both worlds.

**Jupiter** is another resort destination, made the more popular by
association with its local son, Burt Reynolds. The Burt Reynolds
Ranch and Mini Petting Farm are part of his Horse Ranch and Feed
Store Complex. Much of the history of Jupiter is illustrated by the
Loxahatchee Historical Society. They run the **Jupiter Lighthouse**,
the **Loxahatchee Historical Museum**, and the pioneering era
**DuBois House**. The museum is in Burt Reynolds Park, a short detour
south on US 1 before crossing Jupiter Inlet for those driving north on

*Modern Seminole
patchwork*

*The Louis XVI salon
in the Flagler Home
and Museum*

the A1A. Jupiter's association with the star is proven by a pair of his best boots on display, worn when filming locally. The museum provides opening times and information on the other two sites.

## Jupiter Island to the Space Coast

It is said that the millionaires of Jupiter Island want tourists like an orange grower wants sharp frosts. All sorts of political machinations have been hinted at; questioning why their stretch of coastal highway is route 707, and not the A1A like the rest of Florida. Visitors driving north along the coast should turn right onto the 707 just beyond Jupiter Inlet, which is the mouth of the Loxahatchee River.

Beyond Jupiter Inlet Colony the barrier island becomes narrow, with just enough room for a house on either side of the road. A stop at Blowing Rocks Park shows that the site is great for fishing and photography, but swimming is dangerous (and prohibited). **Hobe Sound National Wildlife Refuge** is on Jupiter Island, found by going due north instead of taking Florida 707 inland. The road is a dead end, but the refreshingly natural refuge has a pristine beach and nature walks.

**Jonathan Dickinson State Park** is on Highway 1, just south of where the 707 returns to the mainland. This 10,328 acre park was named after a Quaker who, with his family, was shipwrecked nearby in 1696. The park preserves the upper reaches of the Loxahatchee River, and offers canoe rentals to enjoy the water. Boat trips are provided, given sufficient numbers, up to the notorious site of Trapper Nelson. Around 1936 the 'Wild Man of the Loxahatchee' set up camp along the river, and tourists would flock to see the zoo of creatures he collected. Tours were halted when one group found felled trees blocking their way, and mystery still surrounds Trapper Nelson's death. Do not miss the lookout tower, which has excellent views of the area. The park offers cabins as well as camping.

Highway A1A has few facilities between Jupiter and Melbourne, apart from Stuart and Fort Pierce where the highway skirts inland. Highway 1 offers lodging and restaurants, while Hutchinson Island, the long barrier island from Stuart to Sebastian Inlet, is relatively undeveloped. Those persevering with the coastal route will enjoy it more if they pack a picnic and fill their fuel tank. From Hobe Sound take US 1 to Stuart and then pick up the A1A. The **Elliott Museum** has a selection of Sterling Elliott's inventions, including knot-tying machines, the first addressing machine, and his quadricycle, which in 1886 incorporated many features found in modern automobiles. The museum has vintage cars, Americana, and much more.

**Gilbert's Bar House of Refuge** is at the bottom tip of Hutchinson

Island, a short detour right where A1A reaches the coast. This is the last remaining house of refuge, nine of which were built along the then inhospitable coast of Florida as a haven for shipwrecked sailors. The house is a great place to imagine an era without modern amenities, and both human aspects and life-saving equipment are well displayed. From the rocks in front of the house, one can often see pods of dolphins.

At Fort Pierce the A1A detours inland briefly and then returns to North Hutchinson Island, created when Fort Pierce Inlet split the island in two. The **St Lucie County Historical Museum** exhibits artifacts from the wrecked Spanish plate fleet of 1715. The cracker home and replica Seminole chickee are interesting, as is their extensive collection of early photographs which are used to punctuate other displays, such as local fishing and orange industries.

**Fort Pierce Inlet State Recreation Area** has a Jekyll and Hyde personality. The main park is beaches, short nature trail, picnicking, youth camping — in short, a State Beach Park. Hikers and bird watchers will enjoy Jack Island, just north and inland of the main park, which has several miles of walks around the island hammock.

Along this stretch of coast is the **UDT-SEAL Museum** devoted to the Navy Underwater Demolition Teams and SEALS (Sea, Air, and Land), the equivalent of the British SAS. But the displays are not just about war — the Navy frogmen trained the first astronauts, and the development of SCUBA takes an important place.

**Sebastian Inlet State Recreation Area** has a reputation for the best surfing on the Florida coast. Other beach users will be glad to know that surfing and swimming are kept separate, as is the saltwater fishing, which again is claimed to be some of Florida's finest. While in the area do not miss the **McLarty Museum**, part of this spread out park. Their dioramas and slide show highlight the drama of the 1715 Spanish plate fleet, when 1,500 survivors of the wrecked fleet built a camp and began the arduous task of recovering the treasure. About half eventually found its way to Imperial Spanish coffers, and pirates and treasure seekers had a share, but the wrecks were lost and only rediscovered in 1926.

The shore is mostly residential or undeveloped until **Melbourne Beach**, which is separated from neighbouring **Cocoa Beach** by Patrick Air Force Base. This area has been dubbed the Space Coast, offering the advantages of an Atlantic beachside resort with close proximity to Kennedy Space Center. Orlando is handy from Melbourne and Cocoa Beaches as well, which works both ways. Cocoa and Daytona Beaches are a popular day trip from Walt Disney World and the Orlando environs.

# Additional Information

## Visitor Information

Brevard County Tourist Development Council
2235 North Courtenay Parkway
Merritt Island FL 32953
☎ 407-453-2211 or 800-USA-1969

Greater Fort Lauderdale Convention & Visitors Bureau
500 East Broward Blvd, Suite 104
Fort Lauderdale FL 33394
☎ 305-765-4466 or 800-356-1662

Palm Beach County Convention & Visitors Bureau
1555 Palm Beach Lakes Blvd, Suite 204
West Palm Beach FL 33401
☎ 407-471-3995

St Lucie County Tourist Development Council
2300 Virginia Ave.
Fort Pierce FL 32982
☎ 407-466-1100

## Local Events

*Early Jan*
Oshogatsu (Japanese New Year)
Morikami Museum, Delray Beach

*Early Feb*
Flagler Museum Open House
Whitehall, Palm Beach

Palm Beach Seafood Festival
Currie Park, Flagler Drive & 1st St
West Palm Beach

*Late Feb*
Hatsume (First bud of spring)
Morikami Museum, Delray Beach

*Early-Mid March*
Las Olas Art Festival
Las Olas Blvd, Fort Lauderdale

*March or April*
Toyota Grand Prix (Motor Racing)
South Florida Fairgrounds, West Palm Beach
☎ 407-833-1149

*Late March*
Orange Blossom Festival & Rodeo
Davie Rodeo Arena, Davie

*Mid-April*
Fort Lauderdale Seafood Festival
Bubier Park, Fort Lauderdale

*May*
Sunfest
Various locations, West Palm Beach

*Mid-Aug*
Bon (Welcome ancestors)
Morikami Museum, Delray Beach

Seafare
Lighthouse Park,
c/o Loxahatchee Historical Museum
Jupiter

*Sept*
Great America Raft Race
Northport Marina, Port St Lucie

*Early Oct*
Folk Arts and Quilt Fest
South Florida Fairgrounds, West Palm Beach

*Late Oct or Early Nov*
Bunka-No-Hi
(Japanese Culture Celebration)
Morikami Museum, Delray Beach

*November*
Florida Heritage Festival
South Florida Fairgrounds
West Palm Beach

*Late Nov, early Dec*
Sunshine State Rodeo
Davie Rodeo Arena, Davie

*Mid-Dec*
Winter Fantasy on the Water
Intracoastal Waterway, Boca Raton

*December*
Winterfest & Boat Parade
Intracoastal Waterway,
Fort Lauderdale

## Places of Interest

### Delray Beach
*Morikami Museum of Japanese
    Culture (and Japanese Gardens)*
4000 Morikami Park Rd
FL 33445
☎ 407-495-0233
Open: Tues-Sun 10am-5pm, except
holidays. Donations
Gardens, museum, gifts, reference
library

### Fort Lauderdale
*Discovery Center*
231 SW 2nd Ave
FL 33301
☎ 305-462-4115
Closed Mon, hours vary
Hands-on science

*John U. Lloyd Beach State Recreation
    Area*
6503 North Ocean Dr
Dania FL 33004
☎ 305-923-2833
Open: 8am-sunset
Beach, picnic, nature walk, ♿

*Hugh Taylor Birch State Recreation
    Area*
3109 East Sunrise Blvd
FL 33304
☎ 305-564-4521
Open: 8am-sunset
Tours of home, beach access, canoe
rental, food concession, picnic, ♿

*International Swimming Hall of Fame*
501 Seabreeze Blvd
FL 33316
☎ 305-462-6536

Open: 10am-5pm Mon-Sat, 11am-
4pm Sun. Gifts, hands-on exhibits,
special events

*Museum of Art*
1 East Las Olas Blvd
FL 33301
☎ 305-525-5500
Open: 1-9 Tue, 10-5 Wed-Sat,
Noon-5 Sun, except holidays
Tours, gifts, HA

*Ocean World*
1701 SE 17th St
FL 33316
☎ 305-525-6611
Open: 10am-6pm. Restaurant, gifts,
optional river cruise, HA

### Fort Pierce
*Fort Pierce Inlet State Recreation Area*
2200 Atlantic Beach Blvd
FL 33449
☎ 407-468-3985
Open: 8am-sunset
Beach, picnic, hike, HA

*Saint Lucie County Historical
    Museum*
414 Seaway Drive
FL 34949
☎ 407-468-1795
Open: 10am-4pm Tue-Sat,
noon-4 Sun
Tours, Gardner home, gifts

*UDT-SEAL Museum*
3300 North A1A
FL 34949
Open: 10am-4pm Tue-Sat, noon-
4pm Sun, except holidays
Landing craft, museum, gift
counter

### Hobe Sound
*Jonathan Dickinson State Park*
16450 SE Federal Hwy
FL 33455
☎ 407-546-2711
Open: 8am-sunset
River tours, canoe rental, picnic,
watchtower, camp, hike, ♿

**Melbourne Beach**
*Sebastian Inlet State Recreation Area*
9700 South A1A
FL 32951
☎ 407-984-4852
Open: 8am-sunset
McLarty Museum, beach, surfing,
fishing, picnic, &

**Palm Beach**
*Dreher Park Zoo*
1301 Summit Blvd
West Palm Beach FL 33405
☎ 407-533-0887
Open: 9am-5pm except holidays
Small zoo, gifts, snacks, picnic,
advanced notice for & requested

*John D. MacArthur Beach State Park*
10900 SR 703, Singer Island (A1A)
North Palm Beach FL 33408
☎ 407-627-6097
Open: 8am-sunset
Beach, picnic, nature walks, &

*Henry M. Flagler Museum*
*(Whitehall)*
Cocoanut Row, Box 969
FL 33480
☎ 407-655-2833
Open: 10am-5pm Tue-Sat, noon-
5pm Sun
Home, private rail car, tours

*Lion Country Safari*
Southern Blvd
West Palm Beach FL 33416
☎ 407-793-1084
Open: 9.30am-5.30pm (gate closes
at 4.30pm)
Safari, restaurant & snacks, gifts,
picnic, camp, &

*Norton Gallery of Art*
1451 S Olive Ave
West Palm Beach FL 33401
☎ 407-832-5194
Open: 10am-5pm Tue-Sat, 1pm-
5pm Sun. Donation
Tours, gifts, &

*South Florida Science Museum*
4801 Dreher Trail North
West Palm Beach FL 33405
☎ 407-832-1988
Open: 10am-5pm daily, and also
6.30pm-10pm Fri
Planetarium, aquarium, gifts, &

**Stuart**
*Elliott Museum*
825 NE Ocean Blvd
FL 34996
☎ 407-225-1961
Open: 1pm-4pm
Gifts

*Gilbert's Bar House of Refuge*
301 MacArthur Blvd
FL 34996
☎ 407-225-1875
Open: 1pm-4.15pm Tue-Sun,
except holidays

## Tours and Transportation

**Riviera Beach**
*Crown Cruise Line*
153 E Port Blvd
FL 33419
☎ 800-841-7447
Dining, casino, entertainment,
pool, nightclub

**Fort Lauderdale**
*Discovery Cruises*
1850 Eller Dr, Suite 402
(Cruises from Port Everglades)
FL 33316
☎ 305-525-7800
Dining, entertainment, cruise
amenities

*Jungle Queen Sightseeing Cruise*
2455 E Sunrise Blvd
FL 33304
☎ 305-566-5533
Times vary
Day & night sightseeing cruises,
evening meal & entertainment

# 7

# NORTH-EAST FLORIDA:
# THE GATEWAY TO SPACE

E ach year more visitors come to appreciate the unique melange of living history, natural beauty, and high-technology which is North-East Florida. New England and Virginia are steeped in history, but descendents of the early pioneers forget that St Augustine was permanently settled by Europeans long before Jamestown or Plymouth. At least the world remembers that Armstrong's foot, first to touch the moon, left the earth at Kennedy Space Center.

North-East Florida is the region from Cape Canaveral to the Georgia border, an easily accessible region whether from Miami, The Gold Coast, Orlando, or Tampa. Ideally, start with the Kennedy Space Center and then drive north for as long as time allows.

## Kennedy Space Center

The immensely interesting and educational Space Center is among Florida's top five attractions, and is indisputably top value for money. Almost everything is free, including exhibits and parking.

❉   All tourist activities within the Kennedy Space Center are coordinated by **Spaceport USA**. The Spaceport is located on Merritt Island within the space centre, accessible via Highway 3 for those travelling up the Atlantic Coast, or from Titusville on Highway 405 when driving down the coast. From the Gulf or Orlando, follow the Spaceport USA signs from the Bee Line Expressway.

Visitors hoping to see life-sized rockets at the Spaceport are not disappointed. A small city of them tower over the complex, except for the Saturn 1B rocket which launched the first Apollo missions. This monster lies sideways for better viewing.

Visitors may see an Orbiter, one of the newest items on display, when it is not on the road. The massive, reusable Orbiter is better known as the Space Shuttle, which refers to the entire complement: orbiter, solid fuel rockets and fuel tank. Named the *Ambassador*,

## Spaceport USA — Helpful Tips

If possible, arrive early and reserve a full day. Book optional tours or IMAX first thing, and turn up 15 minutes early — everything starts/ leaves on split-second timing. The free presentations cease an hour or two before closing so fit exhibits around them. From the USA or Canada call '900-321-LIFT OFF' for information regarding launch schedules. Space Shuttles are carried to the launch pad approximately 14 days before launch; take the red bus tour for photographs — they are allowed and encouraged.

**Launch Day Viewing**

Spaceport USA is not open on launch day until clearance is given by NASA, typically two hours after the launch. The closest viewing and parking is along US Highway 1, on the stretch south of Titusville and north of Cocoa, or from Port Canaveral at Jetty Park (follow signs from Cape Canaveral City and arrive early to avoid disappointment). Much of Canaveral National Seashore is closed the day before the launch, with absolutely no beach camping inside the security limits (check with rangers). The Florida Welcome Centers provide launch information to passing travellers. Launches can be seen from Orlando on clear days, but the feeling is not as intense.

NASA's full size model brings home what workhorses they are.

The Gallery of Spaceflight is replete with fascinating exhibits, like the actual Apollo capsule which docked with the Russian Soyuz spacecraft, the Gemini 9 capsule, and a piece of the moon. NASA's four-wheel drive moon buggy is a replica, as the original is still up there. Informative movies and lectures are continually taking place, with Spaceport Central ready to help those confused, bemused, or wishing to learn more. Over 250 paintings and sculptures commissioned by the NASA Art Program are exhibited, with a portrait of the ill-fated Challenger Crew taking pride of place.

NASA astronauts say that the optional IMAX film shown on the five-storey tall screen is the closest the earthbound can get to experiencing space travel. The dramatic footage was shot by the astronauts during training or actual space missions. The earth shots are particularly exceptional, and the audience is speechless as they float in space above our beautiful planet.

Two bus tours are also available, each taking approximately two hours. The red tour concentrates on Launch Complex 39, home of the Apollo and Space Shuttle Missions. Included are a good view of the massive Vehicle Assembly Building, second largest in the world (the

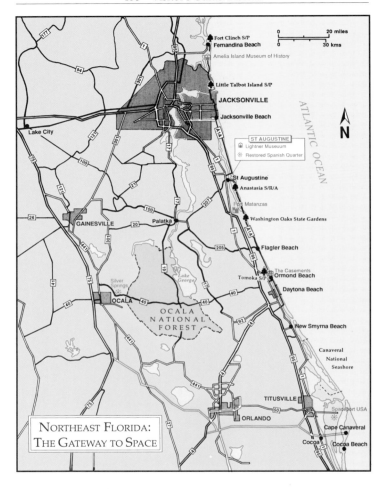

NORTHEAST FLORIDA:
THE GATEWAY TO SPACE

Boeing Plant in Seattle is number 1); a walk around a Saturn 5 Rocket; a simulated Apollo launch in the actual control room; photograph sessions with a Crawler Transporter, NASA's six million pound Space Shuttle taxi; and photograph/viewing of a Launch Pad, possibly including the Shuttle itself.

The Blue Tour encompasses Cape Canaveral including: the history of the early space program; a visit to the site of the earlier Mercury and Gemini programs; viewing the working launch pad of many commercial, military and scientific missions; and a tour of the Air Force Space Museum. Note that both Kennedy Space Station and Cape Canaveral Air Force Station are very active — tours are altered to fit security and launch requirements. NASA maintains a very open, friendly atmosphere, allowing photographs to be taken anywhere the tour goes, with bus stops at the most interesting spots. Visitors should respect security precautions and not wander.

## The Space Coast

NASA share land not used for operations with the Merritt Island National Wildlife Refuge and the Canaveral National Seashore. More species of endangered wildlife survive within their boundaries than anywhere else within the continental United States. The endangered manatee would be in worse peril but for boating restrictions within the waterways of the Kennedy Space Center. Five families of bald eagles also nest within the area, and the once endangered Florida alligator now enhances NASA security.

The internal roads within Kennedy Space Center are closed to the

*Hug an astronaut at Spaceport USA*

public, so access to **Canaveral National Seashore** is via Titusville or New Smyrna Beach. Park Information Centers are found along Apollo Beach south from New Smyrna and Highway 402. This latter, southerly section includes wildlife drives and walks through the area's impounded marsh, flatwoods and uplands. Vehicular access to the Atlantic-swept sand is possible along Playalinda Beach (southern Canaveral Seashore) and Apollo Beach (in the north). Between them stretches 12 miles of sand without a single car in sight. Those playing Robinson Crusoe should bring drinking water, mosquito protection, and remember that the beach gets narrow at high tide if the wind is strong; check current conditions with the rangers.

Sea Turtles nest along the Canaveral shore, laying eggs in summer. Early man knew of them, and the midden at Turtle Mound, accessed from New Smyrna Beach, attests to the numbers of sea turtles and other shellfish consumed by the Timucuan Indians.

**Port Canaveral** is conveniently located for Orlando area and Space Coast visitors. Sea Escape have full and half day 'Cruises to Nowhere', while Carnival and Premier offer longer cruises. Packaged holidays can combine cruising with Disney World, but insist upon time for Spaceport USA, too.

The **Astronaut Hall of Fame** is a new addition to the Space Coast. ❇ This not-for-profit attraction was the brain child of the Mercury astronauts, who have donated much memorabilia to the museum. On the same site is Space Camp, where school children go through simulated astronaut training. Proceeds go towards worthwhile causes, including scholarships for 'potential astronauts'.

# Daytona Beach and Environs

Condominiums and resort hotels rise in waves along the beach north of Canaveral Sea Shore, peaking at Daytona Beach. During the golden era of the automobile, car after car shattered the world land-speed record over the hard-packed Daytona and Ormond beaches. Names like Olds, Chevrolet, and Ford worked in hushed secrecy by night at the Ormond Beach Garage, while by day their cars flew across the silver sands. Sir Malcolm Campbell broke the record five times there, culminating in his 286mph run in *Bluebird*.

Today the Ormond Beach Garage has burned down and a bank has taken its place, although a small museum across the road recalls that era of motoring. Beach speed limits and car access fees keep reckless drivers off the beach, so now bathers sometimes outnumber the automobiles. Instead today's speedsters watch the fast-paced action ❇ at **Daytona International Speedway**. From early to mid-February are the Speed Weeks, beginning with a gruelling 24-hour marathon and culminating in the world's most lucrative stock car event, the Daytona 500. Other races, motorcycle events, and classic car swaps pepper the busy Daytona calendar.

Easter is peak season at Daytona. College Spring Break brings hordes of nubile youngsters in an annual orgasm of fun. The students at Daytona shake off the cobwebs of winter as they meet, mate, and move on. Spring Break at Fort Lauderdale got out of control, so Daytona created restrictions to curb excessively rowdy behaviour.

Shoppers at Daytona head for Volusia Mall on US Highway 92, while on the beach one can find shops, a boardwalk, and a clock tower on the oceanside of the Marriott Hotel.

Day trips from Daytona Beach include Ponce Inlet to the south, and Ormond Beach to the north. The **Ponce de Leon Inlet Lighthouse**, almost a century old, is now preserved as a historical monument. The keeper's cottages are museums, with displays on the lighthouse, a look at the keeper's lifestyle, and a collection of nautical memorabilia. An adjacent park has picnic tables.

To the north is the quieter **Ormond Beach**, actual site of many of those land speed records. Henry Flagler purchased existing hotels and built others in Ormond Beach, persuading his one-time business partner, John D. Rockefeller, to try the healthy climate. Rockefeller purchased the **Casements**, which remained his winter home until his death there in 1937. Now a cultural and civic centre, the drawing room of the Casements has been restored to as he left it. There are tours of his room, which is accessible for wheelchairs via an elevator.

**Tomoka State Park** is located off the Old Dixie Highway just inland from Ormond Beach. On the confluence of the Halifax and Tomoka Rivers, the park offers a nature trail and, for the more energetic, canoe rentals. Sufferers of paddle elbow may prefer the scenic and informative boat tour. Sightings of any specific creatures cannot be guaranteed, but wildlife includes hawks, osprey, alligators and (except during cold winter days) an occasional manatee.

# North to Saint Augustine

The coastline from Ormond Beach to St Augustine is less developed, with beachfront houses and seaside towns interspersed with State and National Parks. Beach access is plentiful at the parks, and swimming is only prohibited at **Washington Oaks State Gardens**, where tortured outcrops of coquina make swimming dangerous. Instead the visitor to Washington Oaks is rewarded by the plantation gardens of George Washington, a relative of the first president. Formal gardens with azaleas, camellias and roses nestle amongst tranquil ponds under stately live oaks, hickories, and magnolias.

**Marineland** is an old timer along this stretch of Atlantic. Dolphin acts are still family favourites, but exotic fish feeding shows, huge oceanariums, parading penguins, a shark show, and a high diving act in summer round off their busy day. Guests are reminded that the Marineland Quality Inn is a convenient stop for travellers.

Further north is where Spaniards massacred survivors from Admiral Ribaut's French fleet. **Fort Matanzas** (slaughter) was constructed on the site by Spaniards to prevent French or British fleets from taking St Augustine by surprise. Entry to the fort, including a short boat ride, is provided free by the National Park Service.

The coquina for Fort Matanzas was quarried from what is now **Anastasia State Park**. This popular beach and fishing park is on the outskirts of St Augustine. Fee paying drivers are allowed to bring cars onto the hard-packed beach, where the long stretches of sand are popular family picnicking spots. The 1565 founding of St Augustine is dramatically re-enacted in the 'Cross and Sword'.

Also south of the city is **St Augustine Alligator Farm**, founded in 1893 and billed as the world's first alligator attraction. They feature hourly wildlife shows, an alligator-filled swamp, a native bird rookery, and a host of exotic and farmyard animals.

Visitors soon learn that virtually everything in **St Augustine**'s history was an American first, including the first permanent European settlement and the first city in what is now the United States. However, considerable change has been wreaked upon that early

*The Daytona 500 is the climax of Speed Week*

Spanish settlement by the British, Americans, and especially Henry Flagler. St Augustine today comprises the rebuilt Old City, the less ancient but equally fascinating Flagler additions, and facilities such as shopping malls, resort hotels, restaurants and golf courses. The Matanzas Bay and adjoining rivers are scenic, the beaches sandy, and the pace of life is quiet or busy as the visitor desires.

Free parking is provided at the Visitor Information and Preview Center on Castillo Drive at the north of the Old City. Sightseeing maps and brochures are available there, as is an overview of St Augustine. Before delving into the past it may be worth exploring **Ripley's Believe it or Not! Museum** just across the road from the  visitor centre, which contains oddities from around the world.

Historic trolley tours collect clients from the visitor centre, while horse and buggy tours operate from the waterfront just south of the fort. Both provide a good orientation of St Augustine, the buggy tour providing perhaps a more colourful history while the trolleys operate over a greater area and have off-and-on privileges.

# A Walking Tour of St Augustine

The **Old City of St Augustine** is best explored on foot, as neither tours nor automobiles are allowed down the pedestrian precinct. The start of the tour, St George Street, is south of the visitor centre. Beyond the restored city gate on St George is a leisurely stroll into the past, with the occasional bounce back to the present. Centuries old buildings in Old St Augustine rub shoulders with handicraft and souvenir shops, but bypassing the boutiques and restaurants is often a mistake. Many businesses inhabit restored colonial homes, great for a quick, free browse, and also try the side streets and alleyways. Overhanging balconies add to the Spanish flavour, providing extra protection from the Florida sun.

There are also innumerable museums, 'oldest' buildings, and tourist attractions. Fourteen St George Street is America's oldest school house. This colonial home was built during the first Spanish occupation; its exhibits include the schoolmaster's life and family.

St Augustine's **Restored Spanish Quarter** reflects the Spanish  colonial lifestyle of the 1740s. The entrance fee includes not one, but several museums and homes. The collection of houses are variously made of wood, tabby, and quarried coquina, and are furnished according to period and occupants. The houses and archaeological site occupy both sides of St George Street, with the main entrance at number 21, Casa de Gallegos. The differing lifestyles of colonists and soldiers can be seen, while guides dressed in colonial clothing demonstrate crafts from the colonial era, adding that extra touch.

St Photios National Greek Orthodox Shrine at 41 Saint George is dedicated to the first Greek colony in America, with a Byzantine-style chapel and examples of Byzantine art.

Cathedral Place, where St George opens onto the Plaza de la Constitution, is used as a market just as it was in the early days of the Spanish settlement. The **Basilica-Cathedral of St Augustine** on Cathedral Place stands tall, its spire visible throughout the plaza. This free 'attraction' (donations gratefully accepted) was built in 1797 with a new bell tower and transept added after a fire in 1887, 17 years after it became a cathedral. This parish is the oldest in the United States, with the earliest written records of American origin.

To the west of Cathedral Place is a most imposing edifice, the **Flagler College**. This 1888 rendition of Spanish Renaissance architecture was once Henry Flagler's Ponce de Leon Hotel. In those days St Augustine was sometimes referred to as 'Newport South', and many affluent families followed Flagler's railroad south to St Augustine and then beyond as Flagler moved to ever warmer climes.

Across King Street from Flagler College is the **Lightner Museum**. This monument to America's Gilded Age was a gift to the city by Otto Lightner. The grandiose setting of the former Alcazar Hotel, another of Flagler's creations, perfectly compliments the museum. Artifacts on display are all from daily life in the last century, and what a life it was. Mr Lightner's collection has captured a rare glimpse of life as a Rockefeller, a Carnegie, or perhaps even a Flagler.

Nearby is another attraction, **Zorayda Castle**, one-time home of a millionaire and a replica of one wing of the Alhambra, 'Spain's Most Famous Castle in old Granada'. The lives of the Moorish Kings are depicted along with their love for brightly coloured tiles and gaudy architecture. Exhibits include artifacts from ancient Egyptian tombs.

Down King Street towards Matanzas Bay and then left on Artillery is another restored section of Old St Augustine. Non-walkers can get there by coach or tram tour. The **Oldest Store** recreates the shopping experience of the old general store, with over 100,000 items on display: high button shoes, lace-up corsets, a wooden cigar store Indian, patent 'cure all' medicines, and even a Conestoga Wagon.

The **Oldest House** is on St Francis, managed by the St Augustine Historical Society. Admission also includes the Museum of Florida's Army, the Manucy Museum of St Augustine History, and the museum gift shop and gardens. The ground floor of the Oldest House is made of coquina stone, and was built by Spaniards during the early 1700s. The British period of occupancy led to an additional wooden storey. Each room highlights a period of the 400-year occupancy.

Avenida Menendez, which follows the Matanzas River, will return those walking to the visitor centre car park. The municipal pier doubles as a mooring for yachts and departure point for the scenic harbour cruises of the *Victory II* and *Victory III*. **Potter's Wax Museum** is inland on King Street, just beyond the statue of Ponce de Leon, who is honoured in St Augustine as the discoverer of America.

Beyond the ornate Bridge of Lions, which northbound drivers will have already crossed, is the **Castillo de San Marcos**. This impossible to miss landmark is surrounded by pleasant parkland and managed by the National Park Service. The Castillo is the oldest masonry fort in the continental USA, and was built after a smaller fort failed to prevent Sir Francis Drake's pillage of St Augustine. The Castillo de San Marcos is now a National Monument, and a nominal fee allows visitors to explore the fort. Views of Old St Augustine and the harbour are excellent from the parapets, while the rooms below contain exhibits of the fort and the soldiers who lived there.

Almost backing onto the Castillo are the grounds of **Nombre de Dios**, site of the first mission on America soil. Pioneer priests planted the Cross of Christianity here; and a 208ft stainless steel one towers over the grounds today. A church, chapel, and Shrine of Our Lady of La Leche grace this sacred site.

## Heart of the Northeast

Inland is some of the best recreation that Florida offers. The mighty St Johns River runs through De Land and Palatka on its way northward to the sea. Two of Florida's natural springs near De Land are **Blue Springs** and **De Leon Springs**. If the weather along the coast gets too hot, or on a winter morning a touch chilly, the constant water temperature of the springs makes ideal swimming. Manatees can be found congregating at Blue Springs during winter mornings, and upwards of seventy have been counted during unusually cold days. Swimming with the manatees is not permitted, as boisterous activity can frighten them into cold water, but the spring head and run are open for human enjoyment. Swimming to the spring head against the flow is exercise; take the boardwalk and float downstream. De Leon Springs has a restaurant where they do all the hard work and provide the fixings, but the guests toss their own pancakes.

Both Blue and De Leon Springs are easy to reach from Daytona Beach and Orlando, as is the **Ocala National Forest**. Facilities range from free primitive campsites in areas known for good hunting and fishing to the popular swimming and camping meccas at Juniper and Alexander Springs. The nearby city of **Ocala** can be found by following Florida Highway 40 inland from Ormond Beach through the National Forest. Ocala sits alongside Interstate 75, making it easy to reach from Tampa and Orlando, but those with more time should follow the scenic Highway 27 up from Clermont, perhaps pausing for refreshments at Citrus Tower. Ocala is famous for its thoroughbred farms, many of which are open to visitors who call beforehand. The Florida Thoroughbred Breeders' Association keep track of the stables open on any given day.

Also to be found in Ocala are other, rather disparate attractions. **Don Garlits Museum of Drag Racing** has some of the fastest cars ever driven a quarter mile. The name Garlits is synonymous with America's largest motor sport, and Big Daddy has been showing his cars and memorabilia to the public since 1976. The **Appleton Museum of Art** is a relative newcomer, but the eclectic collection will appeal to art enthusiasts and the general public alike.

Deepest darkest Africa awaits the visitor to **Silver Springs**. Perhaps it was because Tarzan's death-defying fights with 'African crocodiles' were filmed at Silver Springs that the owners had the idea of attracting more customers by adding such exotic animals as troops of monkeys, lamas, zebra and highland cattle. Today there are boat tours of the springs and waterside animals; a jeep tour through the Florida jungle; plus a host of other activities, including a classic car collection, reptile shows, and restaurants and gift shops. Reduced price tickets are available when booking Silver Springs and nearby Wild Waters, a swimming hole with wave machines and flumes.

To the north is **Gainesville**, arch rival to Tallahassee, and home of the University of Florida. They pride themselves on quality of living, being in an area which encourages enjoyment of the great outdoors. The 6,500-acre San Felasco Hammock State Preserve can be seen from Interstate 75, although it is better appreciated through the interpretive programs. The Devil's Millhopper State Geological Site is a deep sinkhole sheltering flora and fauna normally found only in the Appalachian Mountains to the north. Inside the university is the Gallery of Fine Arts, and the Florida Museum of Natural History.

## Jacksonville — the Last Frontier

Jacksonville is situated in northeast Florida, near the mouth of the St Johns River. This has made Jacksonville an important port, and has attracted considerable industry to the area. Always a busy, working metropolis, Jacksonville has never had to depend upon tourism for its livelihood. The city is rebuilding its inner core, and the twin developments of Jacksonville Landing and the Riverwalk boast good shopping, restaurants, and riverside hotels. Other sights within the city are the Art Museum, noted for its Chinese porcelains and pre-Columbian artifacts; the Cummer Gallery of Art, situated in formal Florentine-style gardens along the river; and the respected Museum of Science and History. Outside the city is the Anheuser-Busch Brewery, which provide tours and samples, and Jacksonville Zoo. Growing Jacksonville has incorporated Atlantic, Neptune, and Jacksonville Beaches, and nearby is Mayport, a large naval port which conducts tours of the aircraft carriers when they are at home.

Hidden beyond Jacksonville is a coastal region rich in history and coastal wildlife. When Henry Flagler railroaded developments in the south, northeast Florida was forgotten in the southward rush. The barrier islands, scene of four centuries of tensions between new and old world powers, relaxed and grew at a more sedate pace.

On the southern banks of the St Johns River is **Fort Caroline**. Here early French settlers, mostly Huguenots, were overcome by the Spanish in 1565. All traces of the original earth and timber fort have long since vanished — the site washed away after the river was dredged — but an undaunted National Park Service have constructed a replica on the remaining river bank. The new Fort Caroline National Monument is complete with cannon, an interpretive centre, and a video outlining the fort's history. The surrounding area has nature walks and marshland overlooks for birdwatchers.

The ferry from Mayport or a drive east from Jacksonville on Highway 105 brings travellers to Fort George Island. **Kingsley**

*History lives at
Fort Clinch*

**Plantation** is on Highway 105, and may well be Florida's oldest surviving plantation house. The massive fields of sea-island cotton, corn and sugar cane are now replaced by a forest of pine, palm and oak, entwined by vines and draped with Spanish moss. Guided tours of the main house are provided by the Florida Division of Recreation and Parks, and the home's furnishings recreate the plantation era. The household servants' quarters were made of Tabby, an early form of concrete, made by crushing roasted oyster shells for lime, then adding sand and water with whole shells for aggregate. The shells and marks of rough wooden forms can still be seen in the walls.

North of Fort George Island on Highway A1A are several other buffer islands. This section of Atlantic coastline sports quiet beaches, while the meandering waterways behind the narrow, sandy islands support a varied fish population, plus the aquatic birds which chase them. **Little Talbot Island State Park** offers a glimpse of Florida as it was. Five miles of sandy beaches and an area of marshland along the Fort George River are preserved, as is a coastal hammock of live oak, holly, and magnolia.

**Amelia Island**, just south of the Georgia border, has witnessed considerable history for so small an area. Eight different flags have flown over the 11 by 2 mile island, and the **Amelia Island Museum of History** has twice daily tours. The Dorian Dig Room reconstructs a recent archaeological dig, which progressively uncovered an eighteenth-century plantation, a seventeenth-century Spanish Mission, and aboriginal Indian middens. The Galleon Room displays encrusted objects rescued from the wrecks of the Spanish plate fleets.

Thirty blocks of downtown Fernandina Beach have been listed in the National Register of Historic Places. The **Fernandina Historic District** has interesting and varied structures, primarily gingerbread mansions of differing styles from the late Victorian period. Center street is the heart of the Historic District, with some quality shopping in a downtown which has retained its character. One of Florida's first property booms took place on Amelia Island when Union Troops returned home after the Civil War, telling friends of Florida's mild winters. Henry Flagler later railroaded tourists to the south, thus sparing Amelia Island from the worst ravages of over-development. Visitors to Fernandina Beach may embark upon a six-hour cruise on the *Emerald Princess*, which provides live entertainment, dining, and dancing, plus a casino. To sample resort life, try the Amelia Island Plantation at the southern tip of the island or the new Hilton.

Amelia Island Historical Tours offer a tram-based tour of the historical areas, with stops at points of interests. Their route includes **Fort Clinch State Park**, which may also be easily reached by car. The park has numerous recreational opportunities, such as camping, fishing, nature trail, and a pristine sand beach. However, most visitors come to see the living history programme at the Civil War era fort. Rangers are clad in Union uniforms, and the year is always 1864 as they carry out the duties of garrison soldiers. The first weekend of every month sees the ranks boosted with uniformed volunteers, but it is good fun anytime. No matter what is happening in the outside world, at Fort Clinch Abraham Lincoln is the President, and that soldier in blue does not know a video camera from a microwave.

# Additional Information

## Visitor Information

Alachua County Visitors & Convention Bureau
10 SW 2nd Ave, Suite 220
Gainesville FL 32601
☎ 04-374-5210

Destination Daytona!
PO Box 810
Daytona Beach FL 32115
☎ 904-255-0415 or 800-854-1234

Florida Thoroughbred Breeders' Association
4727 NW 80th Ave
Ocala FL 32675
☎ 904-629-2160

Jacksonville Convention & Visitors Bureau
Six E Bay St. Suite 200
Jacksonville FL 32202
☎ 904-353-9736

St. Augustine-St Johns Chamber of Commerce
PO Drawer O
St Augustine FL 32085
☎ 904-8295681

## Local Events

*Early Feb*
Speed Weeks
Daytona International Speedway, Daytona

*Feb*
Olustee Battle Festival
Olustee Battlefield State Historic Site, Lake City

*Palm Sunday to Easter*
Easter Festival & St Augustine Passion Play
St Augustine

*Late April*
Riverfest Spring Music Festival
Metropolitan Park, Jacksonville

*First weekend in May*
Isle of Eight Flags Shrimp Festival
Fernandina Beach

*Summer months*
Cross and Sword
St Augustine

*Early July*
Pepsi 400
Daytona International Speedway, Daytona

*Early to mid-Oct*
Jacksonville Jazz Festival
Jacksonville

*December*
Grand Illumination
St Augustine

Holiday Regatta of Lights
St Augustine

## Places of Interest

**Daytona Beach**
*Daytona International Speedway*
1801 Volusia Ave, Drawer S
FL 32115
☎ 904-253-6711
Open: 9am-5pm Mon-Fri, tours

*Museum of Arts and Sciences*
1040 Museum Blvd
FL 32114
☎ 904-255-0285
Open: Tue-Fri 9am-4pm; Sat & Sun
noon-4pm, except Monday and
holidays
Planetarium, laser light shows

**De Leon Springs**
*De Leon Springs State Recreation
Area*
PO Box 1338
FL 32030
☎ 904-985-4212
Open: 8am-sunset
Restaurant, swimming, picnic,
nature walk, &

**Fernandina Beach**
*Amelia Island Museum of History*
233 South 3rd Street
FL 32034
☎ 904-261-7378
Open: 11am & 2pm excluding
Sundays. Donation
Oral history tours, gifts

*Fernandina Beach Historic District*
102 Center Street
FL 32034
☎ 904-262-3248
Shops, restaurants, boat hire, post
office, churches

*Fort Clinch State Park*
2601 Atlantic Ave
FL 32034
☎ 904-261-4212
Open: 8am-sunset
Living history, picnic, beach,
nature trail, camping, &

**Fort George**
*Little Talbot Island State Park*
12157 Heckscher Dr
FL 32226
☎ 904-251-3231
Open: 8am-sunset
Beach, picnic, camping, &

**Gainesville**
*Florida Museum of Natural History*
Museum Road
FL 32611
☎ 904-392-1721
Open: 9am-5pm Mon-Sat, 1pm-
5pm Sun.
Weekend tours, &

**Jacksonville**
*Anheuser-Busch Brewery*
111 Busch Dr
FL 32218
☎ 904-751-8116
Open: 10am-5pm summer, 10am-
4pm winter
Tour, gifts, free beer & soft drinks

*Fort Caroline National Memorial*
12713 Fort Caroline Rd
FL 32225
☎ 904-641-7155
Open: 9am-5pm except Xmas &
New Year
Interpretive centre, &

*Jacksonville Art Museum*
4160 Boulevard Center Dr
FL 32207
☎ 904-398-8336
Open: 10am-4pm Tue-Wed & Fri,
10am-10pm Thurs, 1pm-5pm Sat-
Sun. Free
Guided tours, &

*Jacksonville Landing*
2 Independent Dr
FL 32202
☎ 904-353-1188
Open: 10am-9.30pm,
Sun noon-6pm
Dining, shopping, street entertain-
ment

*Jacksonville Zoological Park*
8605 Zoo Rd
FL 32218
☎ 904-757-4463
Open: 9am-5pm except holidays
Gifts, food

*Kingsley Plantation State Historic Site*
11676 Palmetto Ave
FL 32226
☎ 904-251-3122
Open: 8am-5pm, tours Thurs-
Monday
Interpretive events

*Museum of Science and Industry*
1025 Gulf Life Dr
FL 32207
☎ 904-396-7062
Open: 10am-5pm Mon-Thur, 10am-
6pm Fri & Sat, 1pm-5pm Sun
Gifts, &

**Marineland**
*Marineland of Florida*
9507 Ocean Shore Blvd (Hwy A1A)
FL 32086
☎ 904-471-1111
Open: 9am-5.45 Sep-Jun, 8.30am-
6pm summer
Gifts, food, &

**Ocala**
*Appleton Museum of Art*
4333 E Silver Springs Blvd
FL 32670
☎ 904-236-5050
Open: 10am-4.30pm Tue-Sat, 1pm-
5pm Sun, except holidays
Tours, &

**Orange City**
*Blue Springs State Park*
2100 West French Ave
FL 32763
☎ 904-775-3663
Open: 8am-sunset
Manatee talk, swim, store, historic
home, &

**Ormond Beach**
*The Casements*
25 Riverside Drive
FL 32074
☎ 904-673-4701
Open:10am-5pm. Donations
Rockefeller room, gifts, &

*Tomoka State Park*
2099 North Beach St
FL 32074
☎ 904-677-3931
Open: 8am-sunset. Boat tour, canoe
rental, store, fish, &

**St Augustine**
*Alligator Farm*
A1A south
FL 32084
☎ 904-824-3337
Open: 9am-5.30pm daily
Gifts, snacks, &

*Castillo de San Marcos National
    Monument*
One Castillo Drive East
FL 32084
☎ 904-829-6506
Open: 9am-5.15pm, 9am-6pm in
summer. Exhibits, gifts, part &

*Cross and Sword*
St Augustine Amphitheatre,
Highway A1A South
FL 32084
☎ 904-356-6857/471-1965
Open: Nightly except Sunday from
mid-June through late August
Open-air amphitheatre

*Anastasia State Recreational Area*
5 Anastasia Park Dr
FL 32085
☎ 904-471-3033
open: 8am-sunset
Beach drive, fish, hike, camp

*Fort Matanzas National Monument*
c/o 1 Castillo Dr East
FL 32084
☎ 904-471-0116
Open: 9am-sunset. Free. Boat tour

*Lightner Museum*
75 King Street
FL 32084
☎ 904-824-2874
Open: 9am-5pm daily except Xmas
Guided tours, antiques mall in rear

*Oldest House*
14 St Francis St
FL 32084
☎ 904-824-2872
Open: 9am-5pm except Xmas
Gifts, &

*Oldest Store Museum*
4 Artillery Lane
FL 32084
☎ 904-829-9729
Open: 9am-5pm, except noon-5pm
Sundays

*Potter's Wax Museum*
17 King St
FL 32084
☎ 904-829-9056
Open: 9am-5pm (9am-8pm
Memorial day to Labor day)
Gifts, &

*Restored Spanish Quarter*
29 St George St
FL 32084
☎ 904-825-6830
Open: 9am-5pm except Xmas
Gifts, tours, living history

*Ripley's Believe-it-Or-Not Museum*
19 San Marco Ave
FL 32085-0409
☎ 904-824-1606
Open: 9am-7pm, 9am-9pm summer
Gifts, parking

*Washington Oaks State Garden*
Route 1
FL 32086
☎ 904-445-3161
Open: 8am-sunset
Self-guided tour, coquina beach

**Silver Springs**
*Silver Springs*
PO Box 370
(5656 NE Silver Springs Blvd)
FL 32688
☎ 904-236-2121
Open: 10am-5pm, extended
summer & holidays
Boat & jeep tour, mini-zoo, food &
gifts, optional Wild Waters park, &

**Titusville**
*Astronaut Hall of Fame
   & US Space Camp*
NASA Parkway
FL 32780
☎ 407-268-4716
Open: 9am-6pm with seasonal
variations
Gifts, tours, Astronaut school, &

*Canaveral National Seashore*
PO Box 6447
FL 33090
☎ 407-267-1110
Open: 8am-Sunset
Beach, walks, picnic, scenic drives,
&

*Spaceport USA
   (Kennedy Space Center)*
Visitors Center-TWS
Kennedy Space Center FL 32899
☎ 407-452-2121
Open: 9am-sunset, 1st bus leaves
9.45am
Admission charge for IMAX & bus
tours
Tours, IMAX theatre, dining &
snacks, gifts, HA

## Tours and Transportation

**St Augustine**
*St Augustine Tour Train*
170 San Marco Ave
FL 32084
☎ 904-829-6545
8am-5pm except Xmas
Off-on privileges

# 8

# THE PANHANDLE

The Florida Panhandle once stretched all the way to Louisiana, separating Mississippi and Alabama from the Gulf of Mexico. Both of those states now touch the gulf shores, but Florida still has the lion's share of pristine beaches. Indeed, glancing at a map of Florida one might believe the narrow strip was nothing but coastline. But that would exclude Tallahassee, the capital of Florida, which sits amidst the rolling hills, under a canopy of oak and dogwood.

The temperate climate, plus the nearby lakes, rivers, springs and beaches, make the area popular with nature lovers. Others come for a taste of the old south, the Florida of the past century, or to visit Tallahassee before following the Emerald Coast to New Orleans.

## Tallahassee — a Capital Place

The Florida capital of Tallahassee is understandably proud of its southern heritage. Residents love their charming city, especially in the spring when blossoming dogwood trees line the streets.

The only quirk is a city with a written history going back some 300 years before it was founded. De Soto was drawn to what is now Tallahassee by the agrarian Apalachee Indians, and he wintered in the vicinity on their stored food. The Spanish missionaries also preferred the cleared land, and when they abandoned the area, so did the remaining Apalachee. Centuries after De Soto, Spain ceded two Floridas to the United States. East and West Florida were respectively governed by St Augustine and Pensacola, with only wilderness between them. Travel between the two was fraught with danger, so central Tallahassee was selected as site of a new capital. The legislature met in a log cabin while the city was being built. The name is Apalachee, and means 'land of old fields', 'abandoned village', or 'old town' — all of which apply to Tallahassee.

Most visitors start at the **Capitol Complex**. Car parks and meters ❉

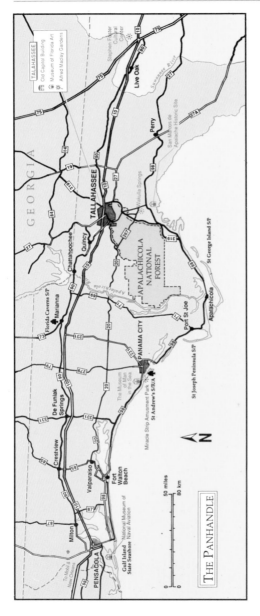

may be found in the area delimited by Monroe, Bronough, College, and Gaines streets. The Old Capitol has been restored to its 1902 grandeur, with its dome and cupola crowningthe candy-striped awnings which shade the windows. Inside is a self-guided walking tour and a gift shop with crafts and books on Florida.

Behind the Old Capitol, dwarfing all else, is the 22-storey New Capitol. The visitor centre at the rear provides free tours, including ground floor art exhibits and the 5th floor legislative chambers (Senate and Representatives). The views from the twenty-second storey are magnificent; quite worth a fast elevator trip for those without time to tour. The park-like atmosphere of Tallahassee is very apparent from the top — the oaks do not just line the streets, they hide the houses. Without the universities and white government offices, Tallahassee would be a suburban extension to the nearby Apalachicola National Forest.

The R.A. Gray building is on Bronough Street, two blocks behind the New Capitol. The **Museum of Florida History** there provides a summary of Florida's hectic history. Interesting exhibits include a prehistoric mastodon recovered from nearby Wakulla Spring, a walk through a section of a paddle wheeler, portraits of Seminole Indians active for and against the United States, and a dynamic, hands-on model of Florida's changing ocean levels.

On the corner of College and Park Avenues is the Tallahassee Convention & Visitors Bureau. They provide maps, including the route of the free trolley tour, and information on cultural events. Check with them for opening times of the Governor's Mansion.

Lake Jackson Mounds Archaeological Site was home to the Southern Cult, or mound building Indians. Today the area has a pleasant picnic spot with a nature trail, but for a better understanding of the Indians up to the Spanish mission period, visit the **San Luis Archaeological Site**. Excavations include the mission (friary, church, and

*The Capitol Complex, Tallahassee*   *Indian craft fair at Tallahassee*

cemetery), Spanish fort, several Indian villages, and the Apalachee council house. The former James Messer mansion in the grounds has artifacts from several sites. The grounds are a popular place for strollers and picnickers.

Just north of Tallahassee is **Alfred Maclay State Gardens**, with over 160 exotic species of plants and shrubs — a unique blend of native and exotic plants surrounding a quiet lakeside setting. Late December to early May witnesses the most prolific flowering, but the gardens may be enjoyed year-round for picnicking, strolling, and in summer, a cooling dip in the lake.

**Lafayette Vineyards and Winery** produce white and light red wines, with free tours of their estate. The land itself was part of a deed to Lafayette in recognition of his outstanding services to America during the Revolutionary War.

## Tallahassee Day Trips

**Wakulla Springs State Park** is just off Highway 61. The freshwater spring was considered the world's largest when output reached 1,250 million gallons per day during a 1973 peak. However, the flow rate at Wakulla Springs varies considerably, and divers have partially explored the vast underwater caverns to discover why. The well-preserved skeleton of a great mastodon was recovered during an earlier foray. Almost 2 miles of caverns were charted, but they still do not know where the water comes from. Park guests can get exciting views of the spring from the glass-bottom boat. The half-hour tour takes in the spring head and the wildlife of the Cypress-lined waterway. Swimming is popular in summer, and visitors can chose between picnicking or the conference centre dining room (park entrance is free for diners or conference delegates).

The Navarez expedition reached the Gulf at the site of present day **Saint Marks**, and later Spaniards built a fort at the confluence of the St Marks and Wakulla River, 4 miles from the Gulf. The **San Marcos de Apalache State Historic Site** recounts the region's history in a rather unusual fashion. A grey, concrete museum sits upon the foundations of a nineteenth-century marine hospital, which in turn borrowed materials from the historic forts: Civil War, Seminole War, British occupation, and both Spanish periods. Museum exhibits likewise peel back the eras like an onion, from the near past to the first paleo-Indians, before sending visitors out to stroll amongst eroding ramparts, mote, and bombproofs. Across the river from the fort is the St Marks National Wildlife Refuge, found east on Highway 98.

A 16 mile (26km) trail links Tallahassee to St Marks. St Marks has no return bus so the walk must be a round-trip, doubling the trek.

Those with transportation can drive to St Marks, visit the historic site, and then walk a portion of the trail. Contact the San Marcos Historic Site for more information about the weekend bike concession at the Tallahassee trail head. San Marcos also provide information on **Natural Bridge Battlefield State Historic Site**, where hastily assembled Confederate forces prevented Union soldiers from taking Tallahassee. Reenactments of the battle take place in early March.

Tallahassee sits on the northeastern border of the Apalachicola National Forest. Fishing and hunting are popular, as is canoeing the Ochlockonee River which runs through it. Two other rivers popular with canoeists are the Apalachicola and Blackwater further to the west. Interested canoeists should contact the Florida Association of Canoe Liveries & Outfitters. The Suwannee River was made famous in song by Stephen Foster, and makes a great day trip by car from Tallahassee, or a lazy canoe trip downstream. The **Suwannee River State Park** is a nature-lovers paradise, with almost 2,000 acres of land to enjoy, plus the river. Just beyond is the **Stephen Foster Culture Center**, which honours the composer by preserving the crafts, music, and times of early Florida. Contact the culture centre beforehand for details of special events and festivals.

**Florida Caverns State Park** is just outside Marianna, a short excursion from Tallahassee. The extensive caverns have beautifully formed stone curtains and reflective pools, in addition to stalactites and stalagmites. While not so grand a scale as Carlsbad, Florida Caverns is still active — the stones glisten like polished marble. The surrounding grounds have nature trails. A section of the park is used by the Marianna Golf Club, and non-members can bring their own clubs or rent a set. Camping and horse riding are other popular activities — but visitors have to supply equipment and/or horses.

Nearby **Torreya State Park** was named after the rare torreya tree, a member of the yew family. Florida's most dramatic landscape is there, a tall bluff overlooking the Apalachicola River. While no Grand Canyon, it makes a perfect backdrop for ranger-conducted tours of the antebellum Gregory House. Walks vary from a short trip to the remains of Confederate gun emplacements to a 7-mile loop trail full of deer and other wildlife. Picnicking and camping are other activities, and rangers will point out the few remaining torreya yews.

# The Panhandle Coast to Pensacola

US Highway 98 is the coastal route along the panhandle, with diversions where 98 strays inland. From St Marks westward there are few large towns along the coast before Panama City Beach. Bright lights and a beach with nightlife is reached quickest from Tallahassee

*Sunset over the Suwannee River*

*Rangers and volunteers re-enact the Civil War battle at Natural Bridge*

by following Interstate 10 and then Highway 231 south.

For those taking Highway 98, the first section of coastline is hidden behind a curtain of pine and palmetto. The Gulf can be seen from quaint fishing villages, where the catch of the day is available from roadside stalls, oyster bars, and seafood diners. Beach access is available at Carrabelle Beach, where there are free parking, picnic tables, and changing facilities/rest rooms.

For a close-up view of a barrier island, take the toll bridge at Eastpoint to St George Island. The sand washed along the Gulf of Mexico coast is still piling up around Apalachicola Bay. The island moves slowly each year, unless accelerated by a hurricane, and yet real estate is big business here. Of course many of the stilt houses are summer homes. Weekend, weekly, and monthly rentals are available, low in the cool winter months with prices peaking in summer.

The nine-mile long eastern tip forms **St George Island State Park**, which faces both the Gulf of Mexico and Apalachicola Bay. Wild dunes of sugar-coloured sand are held together by waving flags of sea-oats, making a scenic backdrop for beach-side activities and picnicking. The pristine, uncrowded beaches make for a relaxing stroll. Energetic tenters may enjoy the primitive camping area, a mile walk from the main campsite with all its amenities.

Across the Gorrie Bridge on the mainland is Apalachicola. In the 1830s this town was a major port on the Gulf of Mexico, shipping cotton grown on the rich floodplains. A physician named John Gorrie arrived there in 1833 and became heavily involved in many aspects of this fast growing town. The **John Gorrie State Museum** remembers this little known man who, while trying to cool patients dying of yellow fever, invented the forerunner to modern air conditioning and incidentally created a machine for making ice. Dr Gorrie died before he could get financial backing for his inventions, but the museum has artifacts and a replica of his ice-making machine.

Timber, and more recently fishing, replaced the cotton industry. The Apalachicola of today is a commercial fishing bayside town with small seafood restaurants and a historic area surrounding the John Gorrie Museum on 6th Street. Several of the interesting nineteenth-century houses were owned by cotton and timber magnates.

Highway 98 diverges from the coast after Apalachicola, and those who missed St George Island may wish to travel down Florida 30 to **St Joseph Peninsula State Park**. Again the beaches have a wind-blown, natural setting, and those without tents or motorhome may book cabins. The town of Port St Joe was intended to rival Apalachicola, and enjoyed a brief period between boom and bust when it hosted the Constitution Convention, a period recalled at the

State Historic Museum. Tyndall Air Force Base dominates much of the coast before US Highway 98 detours inland through Panama City, which despite its exotic name is mainly an industrialized port.

# The Emerald Coast

Superlatives fall short of the mark when describing the coastline from Panama City Beach to Pensacola. One of Florida's best kept secrets is their hundred miles of pure white, icing sugar sand, where sun glasses are essential. The only misnomer is the name *Emerald Coast*. From the water's edge the tropical colours blend from aquamarine to topaz to azure, with deeper waters approaching cobalt.

**Panama City Beach** immodestly claim to have the best beach in the world. This lively summer resort has something for all the family, especially the young and energetic. Apart from the simpler pleasure of simmering gently on the wide white beaches are a host of water sports: water skiing, jet-skiing, parascending, wind surfing, boat cruises, and innumerable power and sail driven charter boats.

The summer influx of vacationers from Georgia and Alabama have earned the area the nickname of 'Redneck Riviera'. Resort hotels line the beach; nightclubs and seafood restaurants fill the evenings, while amusement parks and crazy golf vie for tourists. Winter is the quiet season, with cost-conscious snowbirds enjoying lower prices and the slower pace of the Panhandle. Locals recommend spring and autumn on the Emerald Coast, missing the summer prices but enjoying summer weather and water temperatures.

✳ The **Miracle Strip Amusement Park**, popular with young and old for 30 years, is impossible to miss. The park's theme is simple; good old-fashioned fun on dozens of rides and games of chance. Water is the **Shipwreck Island** theme: choose between fast and furious flumes or a gentle paddle down 'the lazy river'. Combination and seasonal passes are available for both attractions, from April to Labor Day, after which the parks close. **Gulf World** is another popular attraction, where visitors are entertained by the antics of dolphins and sea lions, or stroll through the gardens and talk to parrots.

♣ Those who find the excitement a bit much can retreat to **St Andrews State Recreation Area**. Young children and non-swimmers may paddle in the calm, shallow water behind the jetty. To avoid sunburn, slip on a shirt and take a walk. One nature trail circles Gator Lake and another the Grand Lagoon Picnic Area, with its reconstructed turpentine still. The camping area is especially popular on weekends and holidays from early April to late August (sites ⚓ may be reserved up to 60 days ahead). Short cruises are available from the park and elsewhere to Shell Island.

After a hot day the thirsty head for the clubs, chosing them by the music and entertainment on offer. Alternatives include dinner cruises, such as Cap'n Andersons, and a wide choice of restaurants. The seafood is excellent, and Cajun cooking is straight from New Orleans. After dinner consider visiting Ocean Opry, a country music jubilee for the whole family by a whole family: the Raders.

The Institute of Diving was incorporated in 1977 as a non-profit educational institute for those serious about diving history and heritage. The name change to **Museum of Man in the Sea** reflects their evolving interests, which have added oceanography, underwater archaeology, and marine life sciences to diving, salvage, and underwater construction. Exhibits highlight man's progress from impractical dreams through working diving bells to modern underwater environments.

Highway 98 leaves the coast after Panama City Beach, so drivers should follow Alternate Highway 98 through Laguna Beach and Sunnyside, and then take Florida 30A to the rather unusual phenomenon of **Seaside**. All homes of this newly constructed resort community are old fashioned, clapboard and tin roof designs. The blending of pastel colours and timeless architecture give the impression of a New England Art Deco seaside resort. Nearby **Grayton Beach State Recreation Area** preserves a different atmosphere — a pristine beach with wind-swept dunes. Tanning lotion and picnic supplies can be purchased from nearby Seaside.

Inland from Seaside and Grayton Beach is Point Washington, where **Eden State Gardens** are found. The grounds are natural Florida — tall hickory, live oak, magnolia and pine — decorated with flowering imports such as azalea and camellia. Although the gardens are not so extensive as Maclay, Eden possesses an antebellum-style southern mansion, which has conducted tours, including the antiquities avidly collected by a former owner.

**Fort Walton Beach** is heart of the Emerald Coast. Elgin, largest Air Force Base in the world, dominates the local economy, supplemented by the tourists who enjoy the more mature atmosphere of this resort. **Destin** is the first stop for westbound drivers before Fort Walton Beach. There are a few towering condominiums, but Destin is an easy-going seaside resort specializing in deep-water fishing. The coastal road is interrupted by the Henderson State Recreation Area, and the nearby **Museum of the Sea and Indian** is isolated from Destin by the park. The Sea and Indian is really a museum of a museum, harking back to the old days of beach-side family entertainment. Thousands of shells, hundreds of parched fish and tanks of preserved oddities sit below mounted denizens of the deep. Even the Smithsonian Institution found their collection of Indian artifacts fascinating, and moving from one exhibit to the next may entail walking past crazy mirrors or through a mystery house.

Visitors to the Destin **Gulfarium** get three aquatic shows: porpoise acrobatics, sea lions antics, and the living sea, where a diver points out or feeds 'exotic deep sea species'. Other animals include alligators, otter, exotic birds, and a colony of penguins from the tropics.

Fort Walton Beach straddles the Intracoastal Waterway. The **Indian Temple Mound Museum** is inland on Highway 98. The mound is a grassy hill crowned by a replica timber temple, while the museum next door traces Indian development. The latter Indian phase survived longer at Fort Walton Beach than the rest of the United States, perhaps as late as the nineteenth century.

Valparaiso is inland from Fort Walton Beach on Highway 85. The name comes from the Spanish for Vale of Paradise, although its tranquil, village-like atmosphere is occasionally shattered by the latest jet fighters. The free **US Air Force Armament Museum** displays aircraft and weapons from World War I to the present. Warbirds on display inside include the P-51 Mustang (from World War II), F-80 Shooting Star (Korean War), and F-105 Thunderchief (Vietnam War). Surrounding the warehouse-sized museum are the planes that would not fit, from the B-25 Flying Fortress to the recently retired spy-in-the-sky, the Blackbird.

Elgin AFB also owns parts of Santa Rosa Island, so coastbound drivers must detour inland on Highway 98 until Navarre. Florida 399 crosses a toll bridge to Santa Rosa Island, and beyond the developed coastline is a long stretch of the **Gulf Islands National Seashore**. This national park preserves historic fortifications of the Gulf Coastal Defense System, simultaneously protecting large sections of barrier coastline in Florida and Mississippi. This first eastern section is free, with parking, picnicking, and pristine beaches.

**Fort Pickens** is at the western end of Santa Rosa Island, beyond the turn off for Pensacola. The national park's fee includes access to the five-pointed fort, a museum which encompasses barrier island ecosystems and the fort's history, and miles of undeveloped beach. Fort Pickens survived a Confederate bombardment during the Civil War, but time is the new enemy, and several areas of the fort are closed.

Sandwiched between the sections of National Seashore on Santa Rosa is Pensacola Beach, with a water park and other seaside activities. The first bridge inland takes one through Gulf Breeze, a popular resort community with canals alongside luxury homes for mooring the family yacht. East on Highway 98 is the Gulf Breeze Zoo and nearby Wildlife Rescue and Sanctuary.

*Messing about in boats at Pensacola marina*

*Pensacola's museums relive history*

# Pensacola

Inland from Gulf Stream and the national seashore is **Pensacola**. The Convention and Visitor Information Center, conveniently located adjacent to the bridge, provides maps and information on seasonal festivities, many of which focus on historic aspects of the city.

The Spanish first attempted to settle Pensacola in 1559, six years before St Augustine. Abandoned due to storms and infrequent supplies, it was resettled in 1698. The location occasioned numerous setbacks, with a tug of war between Spain, France, and Britain. The contestants changed with time, and Pensacola saw conflict between the United States and Spain, and later the Confederacy.

Given the city's history, it is hardly surprising that Pensacola is peppered with old forts and is currently home to a large navy base. Pensacola US Naval Air Station houses the fascinating and free **US Naval Aviation Museum**. On display are prototypes of some of the latest in fighter technology, but more interesting to many are the older planes. The NC-4 flying boat, first across the Atlantic, is an impossible to miss corrugated bathtub with vast outstretched pinions. Aircraft and supporting exhibits are grouped logically by conflict, while larger aircraft are displayed outdoors.

Also at the Naval Air Station is **Fort Barrancas**, another coastal fortification operated by the National Park Service. Fort Pickens may be seen from this smaller fort, but the third fort in the triangular defence system of Pensacola no longer exists. The barrier island moved out from beneath it, and the old fort is now a waterway. Fort Barrancas is free, and the Park Service provides a small interpretive centre with a presentation outlining its history.

Further southeast of the Naval Air Station is **Big Lagoon State Recreation Area**, ideal for bird watchers and nature lovers as it is situated along the Intracoastal Waterway. Wading birds may be seen from the boardwalk and lagoon observation tower, while wooded areas sport cardinals, towhees, and other colourful birds. Swimming, picnicking, and camping are available, while their nearby neighbour, Perdido Key, has the Gulf Coast beach.

Pensacola offers more than airplanes and beaches; the city boasts two historic districts plus one preservation area. **Seville Square Historic District** is the best known and the oldest, where streets have names from the second Spanish occupation, but follow the plan laid out earlier by the British. **Historic Pensacola Village** has the largest collection of museums, homes, and memorabilia around Seville Square. One admission charge gives access to their eleven domains, including archaeological exhibits of the British occupation and several buildings dating from the second Spanish period. Tickets may be purchased in the Museum of Commerce off Zaragoza and Barracks Street, or at the **T.T. Wentworth Jr Florida State Museum**, whose extravagant renaissance architecture is almost worthy of Mr Flagler himself. The 1805 Julee Cottage dates from the Spanish period. Just an old wooden building outside, the cottage was home to an early Black freewoman and now remembers the 'Blacks in West Florida' from the slave era to recent times.

Before their numbers expanded the Episcopalians worshipped at nearby **Old Christ Church**. The 'Norman Revival Gothic' structure has been a museum and archive since 1960, organized by the Pensacola Historical Society. Where the pews once stood are displays and artifacts of old Pensacola, while the rear houses the research library.

The **Palafox Historic District** was the business centre of Pensacola at the turn of the century. Although not on the National Register of Historic Places, Pensacola wish to preserve this old example of 'downtown' for future generations of Americans whose only experience will be the shopping mall.

Cultured travellers may check the concert schedule for the **Saenger Theater** while at the visitor centre. The varied calender includes and concerts. The theatre itself contains Baroque and Renaissance elements common to New Orleans. Down Palafox Street from the theatre is Plaza Ferdinand VII. In this National Historic Site the British drilled Indian and Negro troops during the war of 1812. Andrew Jackson formally received Florida from Spain at the plaza, making La Florida a possession of the United States.

Few of the homes in the **North Hill Preservation District** are open to the public, but the area makes an enjoyable stroll or car tour. The **Christ Episcopal Church** was built after the Old Christ Church became too small. It has a rather rare architecture for present-day Florida. The 1902 Mission Revival church was styled after the Spanish Colonial Churches, and forms a large, elaborate cross. The design was chosen to commemorate the Spanish heritage of Pensacola, and for its practicality in the Florida Climate. Apart from attending the Wednesday or Sunday services, the building is often closed. The **Hopkins' House** may not be mentioned in the Historical Guide to Pensacola, but this boarding house is mighty popular during meal times. Anyone willing to jostle elbows with a stranger can sample their home-cooked meal of the day in a friendly atmosphere. The fried chicken is so good it features three times a week.

# Additional Information

## Visitor Information

Leon County Tourist Development
  Council
Leon County Courthouse
Tallahassee FL 32301
☎ 904-488-3990

Tallahassee Area Convention &
  Visitors Bureau
200 West College Avenue
Tallahassee FL 32302
☎ 904-681-9200 or 800-628-2866

Panama City Beach Convention &
  Visitors Bureau
PO Box 9473
Panama City Beach FL 32407
☎ 904-233-6503 or 800-PC-BEACH

Pensacola Convention & Visitors
Bureau
1401 East Gregory St
Pensacola FL 32501
☎ 904-434-1234 or 800-874-1234

South Walton Tourist Development
  Council
PO Box 1248
Santa Rosa Beach FL 32459
☎ 904-267-1216 or 800-822-6877

## Local Events

*Early March*
Natural Bridge Battlefield
  Re-enactment
Natural Bridge,
c/o San Marcos de Apalache

*Late March or Early April*
Flying High Circus
Florida State University
Tallahassee

*Late March*
Springtime Tallahassee
Tallahassee

*October*
Indian Summer Seafood Festival
Panama City Beach

*Early Nov*
Florida Seafood Festival
Apalachicola

*November*
Great Gulf Arts Festival
Pensacola

## Places of Interest

**Apalachicola**
*John Gorrie Museum*
PO Box 267
FL 32320
☎ 904-653-9347
Open: 9am-noon & 1pm-5pm
Thurs-Mon. ♿

**Bristol**
*Torreya State Park*
Route 2, Box 70 (south on Route 12)
FL 32321
☎ 904-643-2674
Open: 8am-sunset
Historic home, hike, scenic,
camping, picnic, ♿

**Eastpoint**
*St George Island State Park*
PO Box 62 (Across toll bridge)
FL 32328
☎ 904-670-2111
Open: 8am-sunset
Pristine beach, walks, picnic, camp,
♿

**Fort Walton Beach**
*Gulfarium and Shell Museum*
1010 Highway 98 East
FL 32548
☎ 904-244-5169
Open: 9am-dusk, except Thanks-
giving and Xmas
Snacks, gifts

**Live Oak**
*Suwannee River State Park*
Route 8, Box 297
FL 32060
☎ 904-362-2746
Open: 8am-sunset
Picnic, camp, hike, fish, ♿

**Marianna**
*Florida Caverns State Park*
2701 Caverns Rd
FL 32446
☎ 904-482-9589
Open: 8am-sunset, year round
Picnic, camp, fish, swim, canoe,
horse trails, golf, ♿

**Panama City Beach**
*Gulf World Aquarium*
15412 W Highway 98-A
FL 32407
☎ 904-234-5271
Open: 9am-7pm Jun-Aug; 9am-
3pm Sept-May
Snacks, gifts

*Miracle Strip Amusement Park*
12001 West Highway 98
FL 32407
☎ 904-234-5810
Open seasonally
Rides, arcades, gifts, food, optional
shipwreck water park

*Museum of Man in the Sea*
17314 Back Beach Rd, (Hwy 98)
 FL 32413
☎ 904-235-4101
Open: 9am-5pm
Gifts, tours, ♿

*St Andrews State Recreation Area*
4415 Thomas Dr
FL 32407
☎ 904-234-2522
Open: 8am-sunset
Beach, walks, camp, concession,
boat trips, ♿

**Pensacola**
*Gulf Islands National Seashore*
1801 Gulf Breeze Pkwy.
Gulf Breeze FL 32561
☎ 904-934-2600
Open: 9am-4pm Nov-Apr; 9am-
5pm May-Oct;
Naval Live Oaks Visitor Center
8.30am-4.30pm all year
Beach, Fort Pickens, museum,
picnic, camp, ♿

*Historic Pensacola Village*
205 E Zaragoza St
FL 32501
☎ 904-444-8905
Open: 10am-4.30pm Mon-Sat
Collection of museums, gifts,
part ♿

*National Museum of Naval Aviation*
Naval Air Station
FL 32507-6800
☎ 904-452-6289
Open: 9am-5pm except holidays.
Free
Gifts, tours, ♿

*T.T. Wentworth Jr Florida State
Museum*
330 S Jefferson St
FL 32501
☎ 904-444-8586
Open: 10am-4.30pm Mon-Sat,
1pm-4.30pm Sun
Gifts, tours, ♿

**Point Washington**
*Eden State Gardens*
PO Box 26 (N of US 98 on CR 395)
FL 32454-0026
☎ 904-231-4214
9am-4pm except Tue & Wed
Tour of furnished home, picnic

**Port St Joe**
*St Joseph Peninsula State Park
  (T.H. Stone Memorial)*
Star Route 1, Box 200 (Route 30E)
FL 32456
☎ 904-227-1327

Open: 8am-sunset
Pristine beach, picnic, walk, camp,
cabins, &

## Sopchoppy
*Ochlockonee River State Park*
PO Box 5
(4 miles south of Sopchoppy on US
319)
FL 32358
☎ 904-962-2771
Open: 8am-sunset
Picnic, fish, canoe rental, camp,
walks, &

## St Marks
*San Marcos de Apalache State Historic
Site*
PO Box 26 (Route 363)
FL 32355
☎ 904-925-6216
Open: 9am-5pm
Museum, fort, trail to Tallahassee,
&

## Tallahassee
*Alfred B. Maclay State Gardens*
3540 Thomasville Rd (north of I-10
on US 319)
FL 32308
☎ 904-487-4556
Open: 8am-sunset. Admission
charge Jan-Apr
Home, gardens, picnic, part &

*Capitol Complex*
The Capitol
FL 32301
☎ 904-487-1902
Open: 9am-4pm, tours hourly
except noon. Free
Guided tours, art displays, tourist
information, &

*Lafayette Winery and Vineyard*
6506 Mahan Drive
FL 32308
☎ 904-878-9041
Open: 10am-6pm Mon-Sat. Free
Tours and tastings

*Museum of Florida History*
R.A. Gray Building
500 South Bronough St
FL 32399-0250
☎ 904-488-1484
Open: Mon-Fri 9am-4.30pm,10am-
4.30pm Sat, noon-4.30pm Sun &
holidays. Free
Gifts, &

*San Luis Archaeological and Historical
Site*
2020 Mission Road
FL 32304
☎ 904-487-3711
Open: 9am-4.30pm Mon-Fri, 10am-
4.30pm Sat, noon-4.30pm Sun
except Xmas. Free
Tours, picnic, &

## Valparaiso
*US Air Force Armament Museum*
Eglin Air Force Base
FL 32542
☎ 904-882-4062
Open: 9.30am-4.30pm daily. Free
&

## Wakulla Springs
*Wakulla Springs State Park
(inc Lodge & Conference Center)*
1 Springs Dr
FL 32305
☎ 904-224-5950
Open: 8am-sunset
Boat tour, swim, picnic, conference
facilities, restaurant, concession, &

## White Springs
*Stephen Foster State Folk Culture
Centre*
PO Drawer G (US 41 North)
FL 32096
☎ 904-397-2733
Open: 9am-5pm
Suwannee river, museum, picnic,
crafts, music, &

# Florida Fact File

## Accommodation

### Hotels and Motels

Florida hotels and motels typically charge by the room, with a small surcharge for additional occupants. Older hotels usually offer only single, twin, or double beds; while more modern hotels and motels typically have rooms with two double beds — great value for families or couples travelling together. The management can often supply an additional single bed or crib, but this should be verified while booking. Most rooms have private bathrooms, telephones, television, and air-conditioning.

Prices and services vary according to hotel/motel chain, location, the season, and whether AAA or senior citizen discounts are available. Visitors from abroad will find that many chains have pre-paid voucher schemes. These offer excellent value, but ensure that the hotel coverage is suitable. Surcharges may apply to guests in up-market hotels or major cities. Most pre-paid schemes must be booked before departure, but fly-drive brochures often list one or two participating chains.

Hotels and motels with a restaurant may offer *American Plan* (full board) or *Modified American Plan* (half board). Those without often give the American continental breakfast — donuts and coffee — free in the lobby. *Efficiencies* are a special type of hotel/motel room where cooking facilities are available, varying from a hot plate and sink to full kitchens complete with with garbage disposal and ice makers.

Toll-free teephone number for the major hotel/motel chains who can supply details of their hotels are listed below, but before booking check available discounts, and also restrictions if travelling with children or pets.

| | |
|---|---|
| Best Western International | 800-528-1234 |
| Budgetel Inns | 800-428-3438 |
| Clarion & Comfort Inns | 800-228-5150 |
| Days Inn | 800-325-2525 |
| Hilton Hotels | 800-445-8667 |

| Holiday Inns | 800-465-4329 |
| Howard Johnson's Motor Lodges | 800-654-2000 |
| Hyatt Hotels | 800-233-1234 |
| Marriott Hotels & Resorts | 800-228-9290 |
| Quality Inns | 800-228-5151 |
| Ramada Inns | 800-228-2828 |
| Scottish Inns | 800-251-1962 |
| Sheraton Hotels & Motor Inns | 800-325-3535 |
| Super 8 Motels | 800-843-1991 |

### Condominiums

These are high-rise apartments with one or more separate bedrooms, giving greater privacy than one room *efficiencies*. They typically have one or more bathrooms and a kitchen/lounge/dining room area with a fold-out double bed or two. Agencies in popular resort areas specialize in renting condominiums, usually requiring visitors to stay by the week or month. They can be found via local newspapers or 'Condo for Rent' signs.

### Resorts

Top class cuisine, entertainment, and accommodation are offered by most resorts, with enough extracurricular activities to satisfy the most ardent sporting enthusiasts, health fanatics, and people people. Some of Florida's best resorts are exclusive hotels nestled in a pro-designed golf course.

### Bed & Breakfast and Guest Houses

Brought back by American visitors to Britain, the B&B has become popular in many areas, although bargain motels often offer the same facilities for less. Bed and breakfast organizations have sprung up to ensure standards are maintained and to promote the concept, and their addresses may be obtained from the Florida Division of Tourism or the local tourist authorities listed at the end of each chapter.

Guest Houses are sometimes known as boarding houses, and a large network exists throughout the USA. For details contact The Director,
Tourist House Association of America,
PO Box 355-AA,
Greentown,
Pennsylvania 18426
USA.

**Youth Hostels and the YMCA**

These provide inexpensive accommodation for all ages, although foreign visitors should become members of their own country's Youth Hostel organization before travelling. The YMCA is busy, especially during peak seasons, and should be booked well ahead to avoid disappointment and additional expense. Contact

| | |
|---|---|
| American Youth Hostels Inc | or the YMCA via |
| 1332 Eye Street NW | The Y's Way |
| Washington | 356 West 34th Street |
| DC 20013-7613 | New York |
| ☎ 202-783-6161 | NY 10001 |
| | ☎ 212-769-5856. |

**Camping**

This is another popular way to see America. For those hiring a motorhome, many private campsites have full hookups, which include water, sewage, electricity, and a television cable. Facilities in Florida's state parks are also excellent, most with water and electricity, but the Florida Keys should be booked well ahead between January and Easter. The Woodall's or Rand McNally campsite guides, usually included with the hire, offer comprehensive lists of sites. Camping or tenting off the road requires special permission and can be dangerous. Many state and national parks and forests have free (primitive) campsites in remote areas. Remember that in winter campsites fill quickly down south. Not all sites allow tents, but Woodall's produce a special guide for tenters.

## Climate

Southern Florida is sub-tropical, with hot and humid summer days tempered by short evening showers. Occasional cool spells disrupt the generally warm winter days, but rarely last more than a few days. February to Easter Spring Break is the busy season, while the autumn sunshine is more likely to be punctuated by a thunderstorm than a hurricane.

Winter can get cold and rainy in northern Florida, the section from the Panhandle across to the northeast. Summer is peak season, while others prefer the quieter months of spring and autumn, when the weather is still warm and sunny. Tallahassee in springtime is something special, when dogwood trees and roadside flowers bloom.

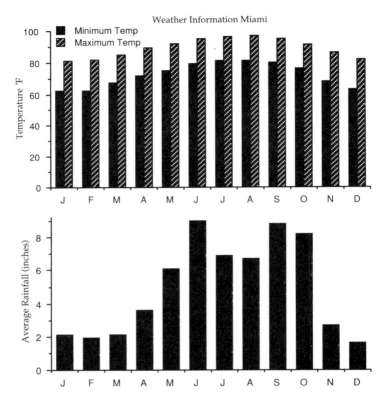

Central Florida has a climate similar to the south, albeit hotter in summer without the cooling breezes found on the Gulf of Mexico and Atlantic coasts. Evening frosts in the winter are not unknown, although cold spells rarely last and temperatures rise quickly by day. Prices are lowest in autumn, but showers tend to be short, sharp, and rarely interfere with enjoyment.

## *Clothing*

Dress is casual; only top restaurants insist upon a jacket and/or tie for men. One or two warm layers are essential, regardless of location or season. Even the hottest destinations have arctic air-conditioned restaurants, hotels, and shopping centres.

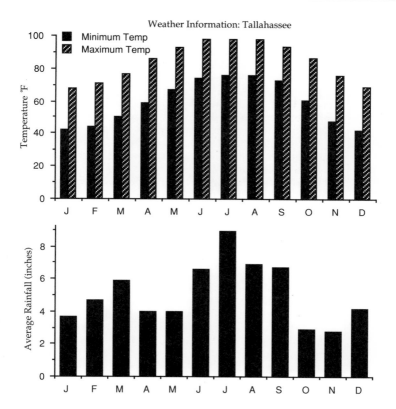

Weather Information: Tallahassee

## Driving in Florida

**Maps and Roads**

For pre-trip planning, the Florida Division of Tourism provides a free highway map which includes major cities, plus a glossy brochure on what to see and do. If travelling extensively, try the *Rand McNally Road Atlas (United States, Canada, and Mexico)*. This provides state and city maps, discount coupons for selected hotels and attractions, distances and travel times between major cities, highlights scenic routes, and outlines road laws, which vary by state.

Driving is generally relaxed and pleasant over Florida's road network, and freeways help relieve coastal and city congestion.

With so many visitors one soon realizes that driving standards vary enormously, and a defensive driving attitude is essential. Visitors may find distances deceptive when route planning: Tallahassee to Miami is over 450 miles, a tiring day's drive but very pleasant with a few days of sightseeing included.

Interstate roads are restricted access, multi-lane arteries through and between the states; normally coloured blue on road maps but are red on the *Florida Official Transportation Map*. Green-coloured lines are turnpikes, which charge a toll but are otherwise similar to Interstates. Speed limits for Turnpikes and Interstates are 55mph, rising to 65mph in specified rural areas.

US Highways are not necessarily multi-lane, and are generally slower than Interstates and Turnpikes. Major Highways, like US 1 which runs inland from the Atlantic coast, are often lined with gas stations, restaurants, motels, and other services. Stop lights often disrupt their flow, especially within cities. Speed limits are typically between 45mph and 55mph in the countryside, 15-35mph in urban areas. Freeways are restricted access highways through dense urban areas, acting as arteries within the heart of the cities.

Road numbering and signs can confuse the unwary. Florida has state highways and each county has its own roads. Signs for US Highways, Interstates, and Turnpikes have a numbered shield with three points at the top, and are respectively coloured white, blue, and green. Even numbered highways go east-west, while odd numbers indicate north-south routes. Florida state and county roads have numbers in a box or circle.

Interstates and Turnpikes are faster than highways, but are typically less visually rewarding. Florida A1A is a highway which traverses almost the entire Atlantic Coast, very scenic but slow through beachside cities.

## Emergencies

### Breakdowns

In the event of a malfunction, coast onto the hard shoulder (breakdown lane), lift the car's hood (bonnet), at night use the emergency flashers, and await assistance in a locked car. If a hire car notify the company as soon as possible and ask for a replacement. PPI insurance, if taken out, may cover hotel and incidental expenses while waiting. Members of an overseas automobile association can also contact the AAA through their local number in the yellow pages or, for breakdown assistance, on 1-800-AAA-HELP.

## Accidents

If involved in an accident, get the particulars of the other drivers and any witnesses. State law requires the police to be notified if damage exceeds a nominal amount or in event of personal injury, and the hire company must always be informed. Some insurance policies become void if the driver admits liability, and saying 'I'm sorry,' could be considered an admission of guilt. Leave medical help to those who are trained and insured.

## Illness and Injury

Medical insurance documents should be kept safe and preferably with the traveller. Call 911 (or 0 for operator) in emergency. Remain calm.

For non-emergencies the operator or medical referral agencies in the Yellow Pages can help the independent traveller, as can an overseas visitor's consulate. Advance payment may be required for those without medical insurance.

While hiking in remote areas, the group should have a minimum of three people so that one person can remain with injured while another goes for help. In the highly unlikely event of a bite from a poisonous snake or spider, always: remain calm, treat victim only for shock, and seek immediate medical attention. Permanent injury from a poisonous bite is highly unlikely, especially if proper medical attention has been sought *without* attempting a tourniquet or other treatment without professional advise. A course of rabies injections may be the outcome of feeding, petting, or molesting domesticated or wild fur-bearing animals. If bitten, seek a doctor immediately.

## Theft and Lost Property

Common-sense rules on avoiding theft include using the hotel safe for valuables, reserves of cash or traveller's cheques, travel vouchers, and airline tickets. Dress casually, wearing the minimum of jewellery. Keep passports and reclaim forms separate from credit cards and traveller's cheques. Lock car doors and keep windows shut while travelling to prevent car theft and hand bag snatchers. Travel in groups, and check with hotel staff for areas of potential trouble (and local places of interest).

In case of theft, report details to police. Use travel or credit card insurance to replace lost or stolen articles. Contact embassy immediately if a passport is lost or stolen, and also for financial help in an emergency. Traveller's cheque replacement will be far easier if the company is represented in Florida. When notifying credit card companies of a loss, most US companies have toll-free numbers, while those abroad will accept a collect call. Several companies offer credit card protection schemes, where one call notifies relevant credit card companies.

Airports, hotels, and restaurants are very good with lost property, but also leave details with the police lost-and-found department.

## Handicapped Facilities

Public buildings, national, and state parks must, by law, provide access facilities to the handicapped. In addition the major hotels and many private attractions, such as Walt Disney World, provide facilities and access for the disabled which are unsurpassed. However, planning is poor in towns and cities: sidewalks are nonexistent and pedestrians must cross at odds with turning traffic. Vehicular mobility is a must for the independent traveller, whether physically handicapped or not, but there are alternatives: join a tour group, cruise on a ship, or stay in one of the many resorts.

Major rental car companies such as Hertz and Avis can provide automobiles with special controls if contacted in advance. Florida produces the *Services Directory for the Physically Challenged Traveler*, which they will be happy to include with their tourist pack if requested. Those visiting Walt Disney World may request a copy of their very useful guide, which includes access information for every major attraction in the Magic Kingdom, EPCOT Center, and the Disney/MGM Studios, plus identifying special facilities for those totally or partially blind or deaf.

## National and State Parks

Florida's 'crown jewels' are on permanent public display. Her state and national parks, monuments and historic sites are open to all. Some of the more unusual parks include John Pennekamp, which is mostly underwater, and the state's 'living history' parks, where rangers dress and lead a lifestyle appropriate to a specific period. For example, at Fort Clinch it is Union soldiers and 1864, and at Lake Kissimmee it is cow hunters in 1876, all adding to visitor's understanding and enjoyment.

Admission to state parks is often 2 dollars for the driver and 1 dollar per passenger, slightly less for Florida residents. Quarterly and annual passes are available for families and individuals using the parks extensively.

The Florida Parks Service may be contacted by writing to:

The Department of Natural Resources
Division of Recreation and Parks
3900 Commonwealth Blvd
Tallahassee FL 32399-3000.

The National Park Service is at:
PO Box 37127
Washington DC 20013-7127.

In addition to the Everglades National Park they operate Biscayne National Underwater Park, Cape Canaveral and Gulf Islands National Seashores, Castillo de San Marcos and Fort Matanzas National Monuments, and Big Cypress National Preserve.

## Renting a Car

Renting a car in Florida is both easy and inexpensive, especially if a few simple precautions are taken. Pre-booking an automobile via a fly-drive package or through a major rental company is safest, especially during peak season when availability is often limited. Rent-a-Wreck companies provide lower prices than major rental companies, but drivers may be stung by high mileage charges or poor insurance.

Third-party insurance is normally included when hiring a car, but CDW (collision damage waiver) may not be. CDW pushes the rental cost higher, typically 9 to 16 dollars per day, but it does insure against damage to the vehicle and loss of use charges. Travellers who utilize their own insurance policy may find themselves paying hire charges while accidentally damaged cars are being repaired. PPI (Personal Protection Insurance) provides additional liability coverage and may pay accommodation costs in the event of a breakdown or accident. If driving beyond the Florida borders, check with the rental company as some prohibit or charge extra for cars leaving Florida.

Restrictions may apply to drivers under 25 years old, travellers without a major credit card, and anyone whose driving privileges have been revoked — they should inform the rental company or tour operator while booking.

## Renting a Motorhome

Seeing the United States by RV (recreational vehicle or motorhome) has become so popular that many Americans live permanently in these mansions on wheels. Hiring an RV in Florida is simple, with similar restrictions to car hire. Both Cruise America and Go Vacations offer motorhomes which may be booked directly or through various travel agencies abroad.

The RV is ideal for groups and families who enjoy travelling together, whether or not they enjoy the 'great outdoors'. These vehicles are far from spartan, offering full kitchens, bathrooms, ample cupboard space, comfortable beds, and air-conditioning. Most come with a microwave and television, which can be linked to cable or satellite at many commercial campgrounds.

The temptation to hire the largest vehicle possible should be resisted. Wise 'RVers' chose a vehicle just large enough to meet their needs — a 35ft motorhome is difficult to manoeuvre in tight spaces. Power steering and automatic transmissions help enormously, but drivers should practice in quieter locations before attempting a major city. Remember that southern Florida campsites fill with snow birds in winter.

## *Tourist Offices*

The Florida Division of Tourism will provide prospective visitors with an informative booklet and a state road map. If requested they supply additional materials pertaining to special interests, such as golf, camping, and boating, and a useful guide for the handicapped.

Florida Department of
   Commerce
Division of Tourism,
Collins Building
Tallahassee,
FL 32399-2000
USA
☎ 094-488-1810
Fax: 904-587-0134

Florida Division of Tourism
18-24 Westbourne Grove,
   First Floor
London W2 5RH
England
☎ 071-727-1661
Fax: 071-792-8633

Florida Division of Tourism
150 Bloor Street West, Suite 310
Toronto, Ontario M5S 2X9
Canada
☎ 416-928-3111
Fax: 416-928-6841

United States Travel &
   Tourism Administration
Suite 6106, MLC Centre
King & Castlereagh Streets
Sydney NSW 2000
Australia
☎ 02-233-4055
Fax: 02-232-7219

# Travel — Getting to Florida

### Air

Millions of travellers arrive in Florida by air. The diversity of carriers, rates, and routes is bewildering, with new routes and packages added almost daily. A travel agent can help decipher the offerings, but some general guidelines may help. Packaged tours generally offer the best value, without necessarily sacrificing the flexibility the independent traveller demands. A basic fly-drive package will leave the visitor with a rental car, this guide book propped open, with the whole of Florida ahead and America beyond. Check before leaving home for hotel voucher bargains, which usually include a certain number of nights in a particular chain of motels at a special price. Those preferring a more fixed arrangement can still see more of Florida by opting for a fly-drive or bus tour itinerary with points of interest, hotels, flights and transfers included.

### Land

All overland routes into Florida are from the north. Interstate 95 is the main link to the Atlantic Seaboard States. Interstate 75 connects the great American Midwest to Gulf Coast Florida. Interstate 10 travels east from Los Angeles, California, through to Florida at Pensacola and then on to Jacksonville, intersecting Interstates 75 and 95. All have Welcome Centers just inside the Florida border and I-75 has a Walt Disney World Information Center at Ocala. Those arriving on the East Coast wanting to go west should take Interstate 4 from Daytona to Tampa, while the Florida Turnpike connects I-75 to the Atlantic Coast — both routes pass through Orlando.

### Sea

Few visitors arrive at Florida by sea, although a travel agent could arrange connections on a cruise ship from the Caribbean or Bahamas if required. Given budget priced flights to Florida, most travellers arrive in Florida and *then* set sail.

# For Overseas Visitors

## *Currency and Credit Cards*

The American unit of currency is the dollar, divided into 100 cents (¢), with coins in the value of: 1¢ (penny), 5¢ (nickel), 10¢ (dime), 25¢ (quarter), 50¢ (half dollar) and $1 (dollar). Bank notes are available in denominations of $1, $2 (rare), $5, $10, $20, $50, and $100. Larger notes exist in limited quantities, but many establishments will not accept notes larger than $20. Each bank note is the same size and colour, regardless of value, so take care to give the correct note and always check the change.

Bank hours are 9 am to 3 pm, Monday to Friday, except national holidays. Visitors from abroad should buy dollars as cash or traveller's cheques before leaving home as few American banks offer currency exchange. Florida has more foreign exchange facilities than most states, but finding banks can waste considerable holiday time. Dollar traveller's cheques are treated as cash, and offer protection against loss. American Express are popular and widely accepted, while traveller's cheques from 'obscure' foreign banks may be more difficult to cash.

Major credit cards reduce the problems of currency exchange and dangers of carrying large quantities of cash. American Express, Diners Club, Visa, and Mastercard are the most popular, although a few establishments which accept Mastercard have refused to honour foreign Access Cards. Non-resident American Express card holders may cash foreign cheques (amount varies by card and country) once every three weeks. Dollar cash advances on a credit card may be obtained from participating banks and affiliated cash dispenser networks, although interest or transaction charges are levied. Certain ATM networks, such as the PLUS system, withdraw funds directly from home accounts without an interest penalty.

## *Customs*

America is very strict on controlled substances (non-prescription drugs), meat, dairy products, fruit and vegetables. Check with the consulate or embassy before bringing firearms, ammunition or animals. British visitors should note that America has rabies, and returning pets will be subject to extended quarantine.

There are no restrictions on the amount of currency brought into or taken from the United States, but a declaration form must be filled in when the value exceeds $10,000.

The following goods may be imported duty free into the USA: either 200 cigarettes, 50 cigars, 2 kg of tobacco, or proportionate amounts of each; 1 litre of alcoholic beverage for those 21 years old or over; gifts up to a value of $100, which may include 100 cigars in addition to the tobacco allowance. Gifts must be available for inspection, and thus should not be wrapped.

At major international airports, such as Miami, there are red and green customs channels. American Customs Officers are not chosen for their sense of humour — adopt a business-like attitude and save jokes for an appreciative audience.

## Documents

### Passports and Visas

All travellers visiting America from abroad, whether on business or holiday, must have a full passport which will remain valid six months beyond the date they are scheduled to return. Canadian citizens and British subjects resident in Canada or Bermuda do not require an American visa if arriving from most Western Hemisphere countries.

A visa may not be necessary for nationals of the United Kingdom, certain EEC countries, and Japan when arriving by air or sea via a carrier participating in the United States Visa Waiver Program. Travellers intending to re-visit America are advised to apply for a visa. Those staying beyond 3 months must have a visa, as must students on exchange programmes and citizens of countries not participating in the Visa Waiver Program.

Postal applications for visas are typically processed within 10 days, but for safety allow 4 weeks. Travel agencies can often obtain American visas within 48 hours, but acquiring an 'instant' visa by personally visiting the United States Consulate General may no longer be possible — check first. The standard multiple-entry visas are valid indefinitely, and will be transferred from an expired passport to a new one so long as both passports are presented when entering the United States. Visas may be obtained by writing to an American Consulate:

United States Consulate
  General, Visa Branch
5 Upper Grosvenor Street
London W1A 2JB
United Kingdom
☎ 071-499-7010

United States Consulate
  General, Visa Branch
1155 Saint Alexandra
Montreal, Quebec H22 I22
Canada
☎ 514-398-9695

United States Consulate
General
Visa Branch
36th Floor, Electricity House
Park & Elizabeth Streets
Sydney, NSW 2000
Australia
☎ 02-261-9200

United States Consulate
General
Visa Branch
4th Floor
Yorkshire General Building
CNR Shortland & O'Connell
Auckland
New Zealand
☎ 09-303-2724

Upon admission to the United States, visitors have a departure form stapled to their passport. When leaving, ensure the emigration official retrieves the form, otherwise the immigration computer alters your status to illegal alien, making re-entry to America most difficult.

**Driving Documents**
For foreign visitors and Americans alike, the most popular way to see Florida is from behind a steering wheel. A valid driving license should always be carried with the driver. An International Driver's Permit is not necessary for those coming from an English-speaking country, and is invalid unless accompanied by a driving licence.

The AAA (American Automobile Association) has reciprocal arrangements with many non-American automobile associations and clubs. Visitors bringing proof of membership enjoy AAA services, such as free maps, trip-kits (a series of strip maps following the drivers intended route), area guidebooks, and breakdown help. AAA affiliated members may receive discounts from car hire companies, tourist attractions, and hotels. (Other discounts are often available to senior citizens, students, the military, and members of various travel clubs).

## Essentials

Travellers taking medication should bring their prescription, which can be used for an emergency top up and also to prove that the medication is prescribed. Replacement glasses or contact lenses and their prescription are also recommended. Electrical appliances must work at 110 volts and fit the US two/three pronged plug. European or British plugs, including 'universal' electric shavers, will require an electrical socket adapter. Drinking the water is not a problem, and water fountains are standard in most shopping centres and parks.

For travel security, one should make a list of phone numbers, issuer's addresses, and identification numbers for passports, airline tickets, insurance policies, credit cards, travellers cheques, AAA or equivalent membership, and travel vouchers. Keeping the list secure and separate from the above items will greatly simplify replacing lost or stolen items.

## Insurance

Good personal health and accident insurance is essential for medical coverage and general peace of mind. American hospital treatment is excellent, but it may be unobtainable unless proof of insurance is demonstrated or costs are pre-paid. Those with existing health problems should consult both their doctor and the travel insurance company to ensure they are adequately protected. Check that personal accident insurance indemnifies travellers against third party law suits.

Injections are not required to visit America, nor are vaccination certificates except where travellers have recently visited a country where yellow fever or similar is endemic. Bring or buy a small first aid kit, protection from Florida's often intense sun, and mosquito repellant.

For UK citizens a 24-hour *emergency* service is available via: British Consul General, Suite 2700, 245 Peachtree Center Ave, Atlanta GE 30303, ☎ 404-524-5856

**Legal Advice**
This is very expensive and best avoided where possible. Purchased travel insurance should indemnify against personal law suites. If legal advice is necessary, check the yellow pages for legal referral specialists. Visitors from abroad should consult their embassy or consular offices.

## Language

American accents vary, as does word usage compared to 'English'. Here are selected British words and their American equivalents:

| British | American | British | American |
|---------|----------|---------|----------|
| biscuit | cookie | cot | crib |
| car boot | trunk | (see also single bed) | |
| car bonnet | hood | crisps | (potato) chips |
| car wing | fender | egg fried | |
| chips | french fries | one side | sunny side up |

| | | | |
|---|---|---|---|
| egg fried both sides, yolk soft | over easy | petrol | gasoline (gas) |
| | | public school | private school |
| egg fried both sides, yolk hard | over hard | public toilet/ convenience | restroom, bathroom |
| | | reverse-charge call | collect call |
| grilled | broiled | road | pavement |
| ground floor | first floor | scone | biscuit |
| lift | elevator | single bed | cot |
| motorhome | RV | sweet | candy |
| pavement | sidewalk | tap | faucet |
| post | mail | tights | panty hose |

## Mail

Post Offices will hold mail sent to travellers for 30 days, so long as it is addressed with the recipient's name and includes 'c/o General Delivery'. Most large cities have several post offices, with only one handling general delivery mail.

Holders of American Express Cards or Traveller's Cheques may have mail delivered to themselves care of *participating* AMEX offices, again held for 30 days. Mail should be addressed to the recipient and marked 'Client Mail'.

Note that some US addresses now have a nine-digit zip code which should not be confused with the telephone number.

## Photography

Film is often less expensive in America than abroad, and most types are readily available. In major cities bargain if purchasing large quantities or buy from discount stores. Film prices increase significantly near major tourist attractions. Many theme parks offer free or rental cameras, usually courtesy of Kodak. Foreign visitors should check that process-paid film may be developed at home. Florida's hot sunny days turn cars into ovens, and can ruin film inside the camera or out.

## Public Holidays

The following are public holidays:

| | |
|---|---|
| New Year's Day | 1 Jan |
| Martin Luther King Day | 16 Jan |
| President's Day | Third Monday in February |

| Memorial Day | Last Monday in May |
|---|---|
| Independence Day | 4 July |
| Labor Day | First Monday in September |
| Columbus Day | Second Monday in October |
| Veteran's Day | 11 November |
| Thanksgiving | Last Thursday in November |
| Christmas | 25 December |

Florida Regional holidays and special events are in listed at the end of each chapter.

## Sales Tax

Foreign visitors are often surprised to find their purchases cost more than on the price tag. State Sales Tax is automatically added when paying and, as if to prove each state's constitutional right to be different, the amount varies from 0 to 9 percent. Florida currently charges 6 to 7 percent, varying by county.

## Telephones

The emergency code is 911, and if that fails, dial 0 for Operator.

All American (and Canadian) telephones have a three-digit area code, and a seven-digit phone number. Area codes are only used when calling between areas. The area code 800 is reserved for toll-free calls, usually valid only from America or Canada. Major airlines, hotels and car rental companies have toll free numbers listed in the Yellow Pages. Long distance and toll free calls are normally preceded with 1.

Direct dialing of calls, even international ones, are possible from most hotels and public pay phones. The international code 011 and the country code is followed by the phone number, minus the leading zero. For example, to phone the United States Tourist and Travel Office in London (071-439-7433) from America, the following is dialled: 011 (international direct dialling access), 44 (the United Kingdom country code), 71-439-7433 (the London number, less the leading zero).

Not all pay-phones are operated by AT&T, and rules for long distance dialing vary, but most phones provide instructions. International direct dialing from a public phone box requires a fistful of quarters, up to 10 dollars worth for a short call. AT&T make calling home easier with their Direct Service. Collect or telephone credit card calls may be made to the United Kingdom by dialing 1-800-445-5667.

# Time and Dates

The majority of Florida is in the Eastern Time Zone, but the western Panhandle is within Central Time Zone. They are respectively 5 and 6 hours behind (less than) Greenwich Mean Time. Daylight Savings Time comes into effect on the first Sunday in April, with the clocks moving ahead one hour, and reverts back to standard time on the last Sunday in October.

Dates are in the format: month day, year. Christmas Day in 1999 is thus December 25, 1999, or in shorthand 12/25/99.

# Tipping

15 percent is the standard tip for taxis, restaurants, and bar staff, while exceptional service or luxurious surroundings now command 20 percent. Restaurant service charges are not normal except for large groups, which then take the place of tipping. Cover charges are not service charges, and tips are still expected.

# Toilets

Usually referred to in a hushed voice as the rest room, bathroom, or often the lady's and men's room. Public toilets are found in shopping malls, large department stores, recreational parks, and at rest areas on major highways (often indicated on state maps). Fast food emporiums are useful in emergencies, although some now charge non-customers.

# Transport

### Long Haul Public Transport
*Air*

America's air network has innumerable routes and carriers. Deregulation has increased competition between airlines, and the traveller often benefits from reduced rates. Numerous airlines give reductions for senior citizens, to whom they offer blocks of tickets for the cost of a few flights. Rules and restrictions change constantly, so travellers considering 'hopping' around Florida or across America should shop around. Non-residents should check for special deals available from local travel agencies, whether a package holiday which visits several American cities or a United States airline which offers reduced price air passes.

*Rail (Amtrak)*

Travellers booking from abroad may take advantage of Amtrak's USA Rail Pass. Each pass is valid for 45 days, is valid for unlimited stopovers, and allows travel on America's largest passenger rail network. From Florida the Amtrak routes are all north bound, where connections to America's West Coast may be found. Restrictions apply, and sleeping car accommodation costs extra. Contact:

Amtrak
60 Massachusetts Ave NE
Washington DC 20002
☎ 202-383-3000 or 1-800-USA-RAIL (from USA or Canada only).

*Greyhound Buses*

Armed with a Greyhound Ameripass and a sense of determination, much of Florida could be seen by bus. The Greyhound (and participating carriers) network is extensive, but travellers may face poor public transport at final destinations, as the Greyhound network is city to city, not accommodation to attraction.

**Short Haul Public Transport**

Taxis are not inexpensive, but are readily available in every city and usually the safest option at night. Most of Florida's major cities have local bus networks, but few offer connections to tourist hotels. Miami has the most extensive network with Metrobus, Metrorail, and the Tri-Rail connections up the Gold Coast to Fort Lauderdale and Palm Beach. The latter is one of the few networks with connections for tourists as well as commuters, with a feeder bus network to points of interest, so long as one has used the train first.

**Motoring Laws and Tips**

The essential law for foreign visitors is to drive on the right-hand side of the road. On multi-lane highways keep right when not overtaking, but many Americans ignore this, and passing is allowed on the inside. Unless otherwise posted, drivers at a red traffic light may turn right after stopping if not interfering with other traffic or pedestrians.

One crucially important law relates to school buses. Whenever a school bus flashes red warning lights drivers going in *either direction* must stop! Children expect all traffic to come to a standstill, and often race across the road without looking.

Radar and VASCAR are used extensively by the police forces. Intoxicated drivers and lead-footed speedsters will find that onthe-spot fines may be supplemented with prison and/or confiscation of the offending vehicle. Especially avoid speeding on turnpikes as the time-stamped tickets are checked when paying tolls at the other end, and fines are charged if the driver arrives too quickly. A new, tough policy on drink driving means that drivers below the legal drinking age will lose their licence if *any* alcohol is detected.

Law breakers apart, driving is actually a very pleasant way to see Florida, and the only way to see some parts. The most likely problem drivers confront is fatigue, caused by the temptation to go 'just a little further'. Rest stops (with toilet facilities) and pullovers (without) are plentiful along the interstates and scenic highways, and regular stops will refresh tired drivers.

Many filling stations insist upon paying before pumping. Lower priced stations, often combined with convenience stores, only accept cash and travellers cheques. Since the station attendant (and customers) would be at risk during a hold-up, chances are minimized by mechanically whisking paper money into a safe. The attendant thus cannot change large dollar bills or travellers cheques — bring small denominations.

A surcharge may apply for using credit cards, and at *full service* pumps a per gallon premium is charged in exchange for a windscreen wash, checking engine fluid levels and possibly the tyres, and a smile. Hire cars use readily available unleaded fuel, but older vehicles use difficult to find leaded fuel.

## *Weights and Measures*

The American system of weights and measures was derived from the British Imperial system, thus they are similar if not identical. The metric system is making gradual inroads, but road distances are in miles, not kilometres. Produce, whether dry or liquid, usually has both metric and American weights or volumes indicated.

Liquid measure differs between America and Britain. 1 US gallon = .833 Imperial gallon = 3.8 litres. Women's clothing sizes vary, with American sizes two less than the British. Thus a size 12 dress in Britain is only 10 in America, and a size 36 sweater is 34. Women's shoes are the opposite, so a dainty British size 4 becomes an American 6. Ounces and pounds are the same in the UK as the United States.

# INDEX

Amelia Island 148
    Museum of History 148
Apalachicola 159
    John Gorrie State Museum 159
Apalachicola National Forest 157
Apollo Beach 140

Big Pine Key 44
    Bahia Honda State Recreation
        Area 44
Boca Raton 125–127
    Atlantic Dunes Park 127
    Gumbo Limbo Nature Center 127
    Red Reef Park 125
    South Beach 125
    Spanish River Park 127
Boynton 127
Bradenton 80
    De Soto National Monument 80
    South Florida Museum 80

Cape Canaveral 138
    Astronaut Hall of Fame 140
    Kennedy Space Center 136–139
    Spaceport USA 136–139
Captiva 84
Carrabelle Beach 159
Cedar Key 88
Clearwater 77
Cocoa Beach 132

Daytona Beach 140–141
De Land 145
    Blue Springs 145
    De Leon Springs 145
Deerfield Beach 125
Delray Beach 125, 127
    Gulf Stream Park 127
    The Morikami 125
Destin 161
    Gulfarium 162
    Museum of the Sea & Indian 161
Dry Tortugas 49
    Fort Jefferson 49
Dundee 112

Ellenton
    Gamble Plantation 78
Everglades 53–67
    Big Cypress National Preserve 64
    Collier Seminole State Park 64
    Corkscrew Swamp Sanctuary 65
    Eco Pond 58
    Everglades National Park 53–56
    Long Pine Key 56
    Mahogany Hammock 57
    Miccosukee Indian Village 62
    Mrazek Pond 58
    Pa-Hay-Okee Overlook 57
    Royal Palms Visitor Center 56
    Shark Valley 62
Everglades City 64

Fernandina Beach 148
    Fort Clinch 148
Flamingo 60–61
Florida Keys 38–52
Fort George Island 147
    Kingsley Plantation 147
Fort Lauderdale 120–125
    Discovery Center 121
    Flamingo Gardens 124
    Historical Museum 122
    Hugh Taylor Birch State Recrea-
        tion Area 120
    International Swimming Hall of
        Fame 121
    John U. Lloyd Beach State
        Recreation Area 124
    Museum of Art 122
    Ocean World Dolphin Show 124
    Okalee Village Seminole Indian
        Reservation 124
    Stranahan House 121
Fort Myers 83–84
    Edison Ford Complex 83
    Fort Myers Historical Museum 83
    Koreshan State Historic Site 83
    Lovers Key 84
Fort Pierce 132
    St Lucie County Museum 132

UDT-SEAL Museum 132
Fort Walton Beach 161
    Indian Temple Mound Museum
        162

Gainesville 146
    Devil's Millhopper State
        Geological Site 146
    Florida Museum of Natural
        History 146
    Gallery of Fine Arts 146
    San Felasco Hammock 146
Grassy Key 43
    Dolphin Research Center 43–44
Grayton Beach 161
Gulf Breeze 162
    Wildlife Rescue & Sanctuary 162
    Zoo 162

Haines City 112
Hillsboro Beach 125
Hobe Sound 131
    Jonathan Dickinson Park 131
Homosassa Springs 88
Hutchinson Island 131
    Elliott Museum 131
    Gilbert's Bar House of Refuge 131

Indian Key 43
Islamorada 41–43
    Theater of the Sea 41

Jacksonville 146–148
    Art Museum 146
    Cummer Gallery of Art 146
    Fort Caroline 147
    Museum of Science and History
        147
    Zoo 147
Jupiter 130
    Burt Reynolds Ranch 130
    DuBois House 130
    Lighthouse 130
    Loxahatchee Historical Museum
        130
Jupiter Island 131
    Hobe Sound Wildlife Refuge 131

Key Biscayne 25
    Bill Baggs Cape Florida State
        Recreation Area 25
Key Largo 39, 40–41
    African Queen 41

Harry Harris County Park 41
John Pennekamp Coral Reef State
    Park 40–41
Key Largo National Marine
    Sanctuary 40, 41
Key West 39, 45–51
    Audubon House and Gardens 48
    City Cemetery 49
    East Martello Tower Museum &
        Gallery 49
    Ernest Hemingway Home 48
    Fort Zachary Taylor 49
    Historic Key West Shipwreck
        Museum 48
    Key West Aquarium 47
    Lighthouse Museum 49
    Mallory Pier 50
    Mel Fisher's Maritime Heritage
        Museum 47
    Wrecker's Museum 48
Kissimmee 111–112
    Alligatorland Safari Zoo 112
    Flying Tigers Warbird Air
        Museum 111
    Reptile World Serpentarium 112
    Tupperware Dish Museum 112
    Water Mania 111
    Xanadu 111

Laguna Beach 161
Lake Wales 112
    Bok Tower Gardens 112
    Lake Kissimmee Park 112–113
    The Depot 112
Lake Worth 127
Lauderdale-by-the-Sea 124
Lignumvitae Key 43
Little Talbot Island 148
Long Key 43
Looe Key 44, 45

Manatee Springs 88
Marathon 43–44, 44
    Crane Point Hammock 44
    Museum of Natural History of the
        Florida Keys 44
    Seven Mile Bridge 44
Marianna 157
    Florida Caverns 157
Mayport 147
Melbourne Beach 132

Merritt Island 136
Miami 20-37
    American Police Hall of Fame 32
    Bayside Marketplace 24
    Biscayne Underwater Park 33
    Coconut Grove 26–28
        The Barnacle 27
    Coral Castle 33
    Coral Gables 28
        Lowe Art Museum 28
        Venetian Pool 28
    Fairchild Tropical Gardens 32
    Gusman Center 24
    Historical Museum of South
        Florida 24
    Little Havana 29
    Matheson Hammock Park 32
    Metro-Dade Cultural Center 24
    Metrozoo 34
    Miami Museum of Science &
        Space Transit Planetarium 26
    Museum of Fine Arts 24
    Orchid Jungle 33
    Parrot Jungle 33
    Vizcaya 25
    Weeks Air Museum 34
Miami Beach 29–32
    Art Deco National Historic
        District 29–30
    Bass Museum of Art 30
    Fountainebleau Hilton 30

Naples 85–86
    Collier Automotive Museum 85
    Collier County Museum 85
    The Conservancy 86
New Smyrna 140

Ocala 145–146
    Appleton Museum of Art 146
    Don Garlits Museum of Drag
        Racing 146
    Ocala National Forest 145
Okeechobee, Lake 65
    Cypress Knee Museum 66
    Gatorland 66, 112
Orlando 93-119
    Church Street Station 114
    Disney-MGM Studios 105–108
    EPCOT Center 100–104
    Leu Botanical Gardens 116

Loch Haven Park 114
    Magic Kingdom 96–100
    Mercado Mediterranean Village
        113
    Morse Gallery of Art 116
    Museum of Art 114
    Orange County Historical
        Museum 114
    Science Center 114
    Sea World 108–109
    Universal Studios 109–111
    Walt Disney World Resort 94–96
    Wet 'N Wild 114
Ormond Beach 140–141, 141
    Casements 141
    Tomoka State Park 141

Palatka 145
Palm Beach 125–130
    The Breakers 128
    Henry Flagler Museum 128
    Hibel Museum of Art 128
Panama City 160
Panama City Beach 160–161
    Gulf World 160
    Miracle Strip 160
    Museum of Man in the Sea 161
    Shipwreck Island 160
    St Andrews Recreation Area 160
Pensacola 164–165
    Big Lagoon Recreation Area 164
    Fort Barrancas 164
    Historic Pensacola Village 164
    North Hill District 165
    Old Christ Church 165
    Palafox Historic District 165
    Seville Square District 164
    T.T. Wentworth Jr Florida State
        Museum 165
    US Naval Aviation Museum 164
Pensacola Beach 162
Point Washington 161
    Eden State Gardens 161
Ponce Inlet 141
Port Canaveral 140
Port Everglades 124
Port St Joe 159

Saint Marks 156–157
    San Marcos de Apalache State
        Historic Site 156

Sanford 116
Sanibel 84
Santa Rosa Island 162
    Fort Pickens 162
    Gulf Islands Seashore 162
Sarasota 80–83
    Bellm's Cars and Music of
        Yesterday 81
    Marie Selby Gardens 81
    Mote Marine Aquarium 82
    Myakka River State Park 82–83
    Ringling Museum 81
Sebastian Inlet 132
    McLarty Museum 132
Sebring 66
    Highland Hammock 66
Silver Springs 146
Singer Island 129
    John D. MacArthur Beach State
        Park 130
St Augustine 141–145
    Alligator Farm 142
    Anastasia State Park 142
    Basilica-Cathedral 144
    Castillo de San Marcos 145
    Flagler College 144
    Fort Matanzas 142
    Lightner Museum 144
    Marineland 142
    Nombre de Dios 145
    Oldest House 144
    Oldest Store 144
    Potter's Wax Museum 145
    Ripley's Believe it or Not!
        Museum 143
    Spanish Quarter 143
    Washington Oaks Gardens 141
    Zorayda Castle 144
St George Island 159
St Joseph Peninsula 159
St Petersburg 74–78
    Boyd Hill Nature Park 76
    Fort De Soto Park 78
    Great Explorations 76
    John's Pass Village 77
    Museum of Fine Arts 74
    Pier 74
    Salvador Dali Museum 76
    Suncoast Seabird Sanctuary 77
    Sunken Gardens 76
Stuart 131
Suwannee River 157
    Stephen Foster Center 157
Tallahassee 153–156
    Capitol Complex 153–155
    Lake Jackson Mounds Archaeo-
        logical Sit 155
    Museum of Florida History 155
    Natural Bridge Battlefield State
        Historic Site 157
    San Luis Archaeological Site 155
Tamiami Trail 61–62
Tampa 68–72
    Bobby's Seminole Indian Village 73
    Busch Gardens, The Dark
        Continent 68–72
    Henry B. Plant Museum 73
    Lowry Zoo 72
    Museum of Science & Industry 72
    Ybor City 73
Tarpon Springs 86
Titusville 140
    Canaveral National Seashore 140
Torreya State Park 157

Valparaiso 162
    USAF Armament Museum 162
Venice 82
Virginia Key 25
    Miami Seaquarium 25

Wakulla Springs 156
Weeki Wachee 88
Wekiwa Springs 116
West Palm Beach 129
    Dreher Park Zoo 129
    Lion Country Safari 129
    Norton Gallery of Art 129
    South Florida Science Museum
        129
Winter Haven 113
    Cypress Gardens 113